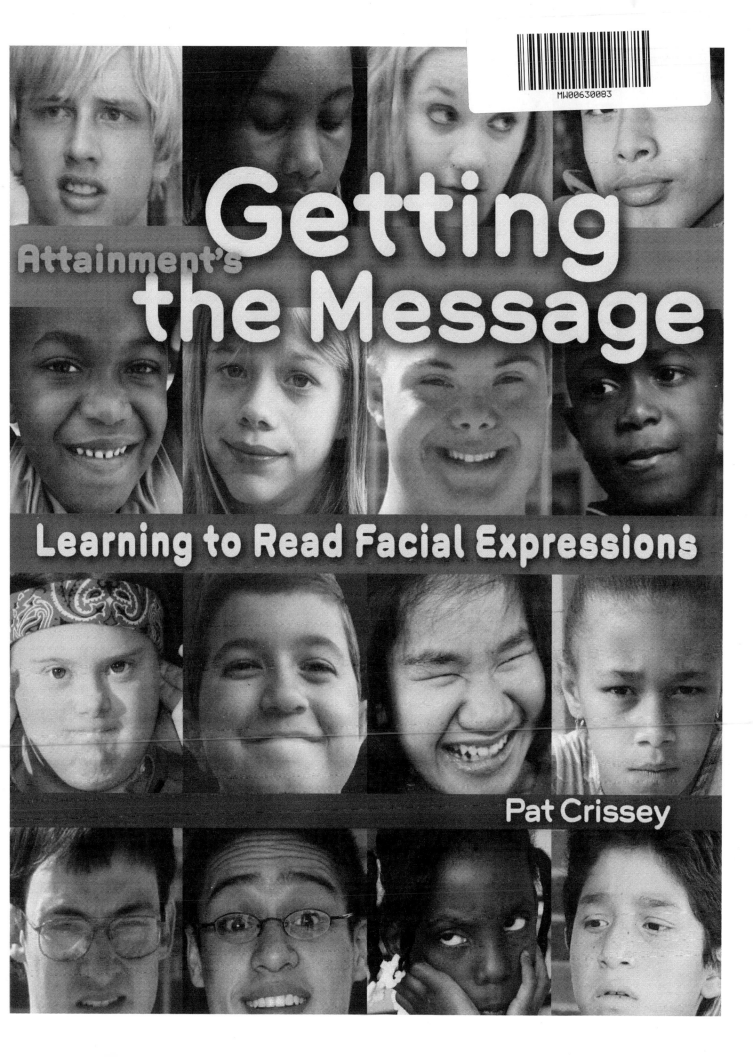

Attainment's Getting the Message

Learning to Read Facial Expressions

Pat Crissey

Win/Mac CD

Included with this book is a CD containing the entire book in PDF form so you can review and print out pages from your computer. This PDF (portable document format) file requires Acrobat Reader to access the file.

If you have Acrobat Reader software already on your computer, open Acrobat Reader, then open Getting-the-Message.pdf from the CD.

To Install Acrobat Reader for Windows:
Run ARINSTALL.EXE. After installation, open Acrobat Reader, then open Getting-the-Message.pdf

To install Acrobat Reader for Mac:
Run Acrobat Reader Installer. After installation, open Getting-the-Message.pdf

Pat Crissey, Author
Illustrated by Noah Crissey and
Soraya Kongnguen Crissey
Tom Kinney, Editor
Jo Reynolds, Cover Art
Lynn Chrisman, Graphic Designer

An Attainment Company Publication
©2007 Attainment Company, Inc. All Rights Reserved.
Printed in the United States of America.

ISBN: 1-57861-605-0

Attainment Company, Inc.
P.O. Box 930160 • Verona, Wisconsin 53593-0160 USA
Phone: 1-800-327-4269 • Fax: 1-800-942-3865
www.AttainmentCompany.com

Getting the Message:
Learning to Read Facial Expressions

Basic Emotion Picture Cards for Unit 2

UNIT 3: Intensity and Basic Variations of Emotions............102

Resource Pages for Unit 3

About the Author and Illustrators

Pat Crissey has worked in the field of special education for over twenty years, as a special education teacher and autism consultant. She received a Bachelor of Science degree in special and elementary education from Illinois State University and completed graduate work in special education from Western Oregon University. She lives in McMinnville, Oregon with her husband, has three grown children and two young granddaughters.

Noah Crissey and his wife, Soraya Kongnguen Crissey, are both freelance artists and illustrators living in Seattle, Washington. Noah is a graduate of the Art Institute of Seattle and has illustrated numerous books and editorial cartoons. Soraya holds a Bachelor of Fine Arts from Chiang Mai University and teaching credentials from Mahamakut Buddhist University. Soraya taught art at Siamand Nakorn Payap International Schools in Thailand before moving to the United States.

Why Teach About Facial Expressions?

"Decades of research and clinical observation have led us to believe that ... the ability to utilize nonverbal language effectively is the very basis of solid and satisfying social and vocational success throughout life; the absence of this ability is an identifiable and correctable cause of social difficulties."

Duke, Nowicki, & Martin, 1996

Most of us are aware of the importance of non-verbal communication. We feel embarrassed when we fail to pick up on a non-verbal cue or aggravated when others aren't aware of what we are trying to tell them with our face or body. Only 7% of emotional meaning is expressed with the use of words, while 55% is conveyed through facial expression, body language and gestures. (Mehrabian, 1987)

However, some individuals are simply not effectively reading facial expressions or are unable to use facial expressions to convey what they are feeling. In a study completed by Nowicki and Duke (Nowicki & Duke, 1989) on over one thousand six to ten-year-old children, only seven to ten percent were totally proficient in reading and conveying emotions accurately using facial expressions. While many children show some deficits when it comes to facial expressions, individuals with an Autism Spectrum Disorder are frequently so limited in their ability to read and use facial expressions that it severely impacts their social interactions.

Non-verbal communication is similar to a language, a highly complex and often subtle language. While verbal and written language is directly taught, children are expected to learn non-verbal communication by observing others. For some children, especially those with an Autism Spectrum Disorder, this can be a daunting and frustrating task and failure to master it leads directly to difficulties with interpersonal relationships. However, while some children have difficulty mastering the nuances of non-verbal communication on their own, all can make progress when the skills are directly and systematically taught. This curriculum has been developed to specifically meet the needs of those with Autism Spectrum and similar disorders.

Where to Start— Assessing Skills

A child's ability to understand and use appropriate facial expressions can often be determined through informal observational assessments. Often those who live or work with a child, recognize the child's limited skills through everyday observations.

However, to gather more specific information, which could be helpful in determining how to use this curriculum, some systematic informal assessment may be necessary. Such an assessment may help pinpoint specific needs. For example, some students may read facial expressions, but have difficulty displaying appropriate facial expressions. Some students may not understand what constitutes feeling sad or angry or scared. Often students will understand and use appropriate facial expressions for the most basic emotions, such as happy, sad, scared and angry, but have difficulty reading gradations in emotions or more subtle emotions, such as annoyed, worried, and embarrassed. Using the following assessment will help you key in on the specific areas that are difficult for the student and enable you to determine which parts of the curriculum are appropriate for a specific child.

The assessment provided is informal, with the purpose of giving the teacher, parent or therapist valuable information. It is not a standardized formal assessment. If more information is needed, a speech language pathologist can evaluate the child using a formal assessment of nonverbal communication skills.

Face Picture Cards and written **Scenarios** have been provided to use both for assessment as well as in teaching activities. In addition, a set of **Scenarios (pages 22–29)** have been included that were written specifically for assessment. However, these scenarios can be used in the teaching activities if they are not needed as part of the assessment. To measure progress, repeat the assessment using facial expression cards and scenarios that you have set aside and not yet used in teaching, or use other pictures of faces you have collected and scenarios that you have written.

Areas to Assess

There are five main questions that this assessment is designed to answer.

▶ Can the student discriminate different expressions and identify which expressions match which emotions?

▶ Does the student display appropriate facial expressions to match the situation?

▶ Does the student understand the emotions that go with the facial expression? Can he recognize those emotions in himself and determine which events prompt which emotions?

▶ Is the student able to read, understand and display basic emotions — happy, sad, angry, scared and neutral?

▶ Is the student able to read, understand and display more subtle emotions?

After using the assessment to answer the above questions, it would be helpful to compare the findings with what is generally observed in the child's everyday behavior. Some students may have the ability to recognize and use facial expressions when it's an isolated task that they are concentrating on, but have not yet mastered it to such a degree that it is part of their everyday interactions. Both systematic and everyday observations should be considered in deciding what skills to teach.

It is often difficult to distinguish some facial expressions, and different situations can trigger varying reactions in different people. When scoring the assessment, give students credit for each reasonable response, regardless of whether it was the response you were seeking.

Systematic Informal Assessment— Facial Expressions

Assessment Data Sheets are provided on pages 19–21.

Reading Facial Expressions

▶ Copy and cut apart the Set 1 — **Basic Emotions Cards** on **pages 57–66**. Sort them into cartoon faces and realistic drawings. Select at least 2 cartoons of each of the basic emotions and mix them together so that they will be presented in random order. Use more cards if there is any uncertainty of the student's ability to read the expressions. Do the same with the drawings.

▶ Have copies of the **Basic Emotions Word Cards (page 44)** available or write the words happy, sad, angry, scared and neutral where the student can refer to them. Tell the student that you are going to show him/her some pictures and you want him to tell you if the person in the picture looks happy, sad, angry, scared or just sort of regular or neutral.

▶ Show the cards of the cartoon faces to the student one at a time and ask him or her to tell you how the person in the picture is feeling. You might also ask, "How can you tell?" to see how aware the student is of different facial features. If the student can identify the emotions on 8 of the 10 cartoon cards (or 80% of the number of cards presented) then repeat using the drawings. You might also want to use photographs. A space on the data sheet has been provided. Photographs have not been provided with this curriculum but can be easily gathered from magazines or commercial facial expression cards can be purchased. (See the list of Resources and Supplementary Materials at the end of this introduction.)

- If the student can tell the correct emotion on 80% of the cards with the drawings, then repeat the steps above using the **Intensity Facial Expression Cards (pages 120–127)**. Tell the student that you are going to show him pictures of people who are happy, sad, angry or scared and you want him to tell you if the person is just a little bit happy or very happy or just a little sad or very sad. Do a few examples with the student to make sure he understands how to respond before you begin the assessment.

- Finally, repeat the process with the cards from **Other Emotions, pages 158–167**, using cartoons or drawings. Assess students using the other emotions cards, regardless of how the student did with the Intensity cards, as these skills are not necessarily sequential.

If working with a larger group, answer sheets could be provided with the emotion words listed on them for the student to circle as you show the facial expression card, or on an overhead projector. (See example at right.)

Circle the right word.			
1. happy	sad	angry	scared
2. happy	sad	angry	scared
3. happy	sad	angry	scared
4. happy	sad	angry	scared
5. happy	sad	angry	scared
6. happy	sad	angry	scared
7. happy	sad	angry	scared
8. happy	sad	angry	scared
9. happy	sad	angry	scared
10. happy	sad	angry	scared

Using Facial Expressions

Demonstrating facial expressions on demand can be difficult for some students, even those who use appropriate facial expressions in everyday situations. For that reason, it is vital to compare the assessment observations with what is observed throughout the day.

- Choose at least two scenarios for each emotion from the **Scenarios—Basic Emotions sheets, pages 80–82.** Use more scenarios if there is any uncertainty of the student's ability to express the emotion appropriately.

- Present the scenarios in random order by reading them to the student and then saying, "That would make me feel happy (sad, angry, or scared). How do you look when you're happy?" or "Show me a happy face." For neutral, you could say, "That wouldn't really make me feel happy, sad, angry or scared. Show me just your regular face."

- If the student is able to accurately express emotions 80% of the time, then choose scenarios from the **Scenarios—Other Emotions for Assessment, pages 22–29.** These scenarios have been written specifically for assessing the more complex emotions in this part of the assessment and the following part (Understanding Emotions). Each scenario presents a situation and asks the student to show how her face would look. Ignore the second part ("Would you be feeling...?") at this time. When giving this part of the assessment, feel free to name the emotion for the student. For example, you could say, "You'd probably feel confused. Show how your face looks when you're confused." (No testing is done on using facial expressions for different levels of intensity, as it can often prove difficult for students to create the subtle variations of an emotion on demand.)

Understanding Emotions

▶ Choose at least two scenarios (which were not already used in the assessment) from the **Scenarios — Basic Emotions, pages 80–82**. Use more scenarios if there is any uncertainty of the student's ability to understand the emotion.

▶ Have **Basic Emotions Word Cards (page 44)** or a list of the basic emotions present for the student to refer to.

▶ Present the scenarios in random order and ask the student, "How would you feel if that happened to you?"

▶ If student responds correctly to 80% of the scenarios, repeat with **Scenarios—Intensity, pages 111– 114**. Make a list of intensities of basic emotions (a little happy, very happy, a little sad, very sad, etc.) and have it available for student to refer to.

▶ Repeat with **Scenarios—Other Emotions for Assessment pages 22–29**, using the question written after each scenario (Would you be feeling...?)

Using the Information

While conducting this informal assessment, look for areas of difficulty and patterns. Can the student identify facial expressions in cartoon figures, but not in drawings or photographs? Does he recognize basic emotions, but not the more complex or subtle ones? How did what you learned from the assessment match with what you observe day to day?

This information should enable you to make an informed decision on which parts of the curriculum to use. While further assessment was given when a student was accurate on 80% of the items, this does not necessarily show mastery. The 80% threshold was set in order to gain maximum useful information, without needlessly frustrating the student. Students do not always learn to recognize and use facial expressions in an organized linear way. Splinter skills may exist. Unless a student is accurate on close to 100% of the items, then those skills need to be taught. However, the material may be covered more quickly, with fewer reinforcement activities, with students who score higher on the assessment.

This curriculum teaches the more easily learned skills first, then progresses to more difficult ones. (See the sequence listed below.) To determine where to begin in the curriculum, identify the first area in the sequence where the student has difficulty and begin there. For example, if a student understood basic emotions and could use and recognize the corresponding facial expressions, but was confused by more complex emotions, you would begin with Unit 3.

Outline of Curriculum

► Unit 1 covers recognizing and using facial expressions for the basic emotions of happy, sad, angry, scared and neutral. Facial expressions are taught one at a time using cartoons, realistic drawings and photographs.

► Unit 2 covers understanding the meaning of the emotions happy, sad, angry, scared and neutral. In other words the student can tell how different events make him feel.

► Unit 3 covers understanding gradations and intensity of the basic emotions and recognizing the corresponding facial expressions.

► Unit 4 covers understanding some different, subtler emotions and recognizing the facial expression that corresponds with those emotions.

Teaching Tips

The following are some suggestions for teaching the *Getting the Message: Learning to Read Facial Expressions* curriculum.

► Before you begin teaching, discuss why it is important, from the student's point of view, to correctly read and display facial expressions and frequently review this information throughout the various teaching activities.

► Use informal assessments to set goals and check progress. Non-verbal communication has not traditionally been assessed, task-analyzed, or systematically taught. However, for students who have not learned these skills, it is apparent that a more systematic approach is called for.

► Focus on one skill at a time. It's impossible to completely separate the different components of non-verbal communication, but try to keep the emphasis on one skill until the student achieves a level of comfort and mastery of that skill. For example, don't get sidetracked with the different intensity levels of emotions until the student has a firm understanding of the basic emotions.

► Frequently review what has been covered and use ample reinforcement activities. This curriculum endeavors to provide a variety of reinforcement activities, appropriate for different ages. Some students may not need all the activities, other students may require that the activities be repeated numerous times.

► Work for generalization. A common problem among students who struggle with non-verbal communication skills is that they will exhibit the skill in one setting, but not another. Enlist the cooperation of parents and others who interact with the student by keeping them informed about what is being taught and what the expectations are for the student.

Independent Reinforcement Activities

Each unit contains activity sheets that students can work on independently to reinforce skills taught. Not all activity sheets will be appropriate or necessary for all students.

Some students may benefit from using a structured learning format to provide independent reinforcement activities. These structured learning tasks are particularly helpful with students with Autism Spectrum Disorders or highly distractible or disorganized students. The tasks are presented in a visually organized, predictable and readily understood manner. The student can quickly determine exactly what he is supposed to do, like how much work he has to do and when it is completed. Structured learning tasks can be provided using file folder tasks or individually created work systems. (See examples at right.) Each unit lists ideas for creating file folder tasks or work systems. More information on structured teaching can be found on the Division TEACCH website, **http://www.teacch.com**

Using Reminder Stories

Some students may benefit from using personal reminder stories to help them generalize the skills learned into other settings. Three examples of **Reminder Stories** are included on **pages 31–33**. These stories are similar to the social stories that Carol Gray described in *The New Social Story Book: Illustrated Edition (2000)*. Social Stories are designed to help individuals recognize relevant social cues and select appropriate responses. Ms. Gray describes in detail how to write Social Stories in her book and on the website, **http://www.thegraycenter.org**

The stories presented here are very general and are included to provide examples of how such stories can be used. To write a story for a student, pinpoint an area of difficulty and build a story based on the specific problem, including an appropriate course of action. The stories can be personalized by having the student write what he will try to do and strategies he will use. When writing a story for an individual student,

Include positive statements about his or her abilities or progress. With older students, the writing of the story could be completed with the student. Pictures can also be added using clip-art, picture symbols, photographs or students could draw their own illustrations.

Stories are generally written in the first person, to be read by the students, though they can be written in third person, or what Carol Gray refers to as 'Social Articles,' for older students. Stories can be read to the student or recorded if the student has difficulty reading the stories fluently. How often stories are read depends on the student, but generally stories should be reviewed on a regular basis until they are no longer needed.

What You'll Need and Additional Resources

Mirrors Mirrors are essential for teaching students to use appropriate facial expressions. Individual hand mirrors are best.

Additional Pictures Additional illustrations and photographs, though not essential would be very helpful, particularly with students needing more practice and reinforcement. As part of the learning process, students can help in finding pictures in magazines, comics, greeting cards, calendars, etc. Supplemental pictures can also be purchased from various publishers. (See resources below.)

Resources for Supplementary Materials

▶ Free online facial expression games are available at the website **http://www.do2learn.com** Look for 'Emotions Games' under the Songs & Games section.

▶ Nearly 300 emotions are shown on the website, Eric Conveys an Emotion **http://www.emotioneric.com**

▶ *Webber Photo Emotions Cards and Photo Feelings Fun Decks* are available from Super Duper Publications, 800-277-8737, **http://www.superduperinc.com**

▶ *Emotions* flashcards are available from Different Roads to Learning, 800-853-1057, **http://www.difflearn.com**

▶ *Teaching Emotions* DVD is available from Different Roads to Learning, 800-853-1057, **http://www.difflearn.com**

▶ *Emotional Bingo* game, available from PCI Education, 800-594-4263, **http://www.pcieducation.com**

▶ *The Emotions Game*, available from Lingui Systems, 800-776-4332, **http://www.linguisystems.com**

Reading Facial Expressions

	Cartoons	Drawings	Photos
Set 1—Basic Emotions			
Happy			
Sad			
Angry			
Scared			
Neutral			
Total # Given _____ Total # Correct _____		% Correct _____	

	Cartoons	Drawings	Photos
Set 2—Intensity			
Very Happy			
A Little Happy			
Very Sad			
A Little Sad			
Very Angry			
A Little Angry			
Very Scared			
A Little Scared			
Total # Given _____ Total # Correct _____		% Correct _____	

	Cartoons	Drawings	Photos
Set 3—Other Emotions			
Interested			
Bored			
Disgusted			
Embarrassed			
Sorry			
Confused			
Surprised			
Concerned			
Total # Given _____ Total # Correct _____		% Correct _____	

Using Facial Expressions

	Scenario 1	Scenario 2	Additional Scenarios
Set 1—**Basic Emotions**			
Happy			
Sad			
Angry			
Scared			
Neutral			
Total # Given _____ Total # Correct _____		% Correct _____	

	Scenario 1	Scenario 2	Additional Scenarios
Set 3—**Other Emotions**			
Interested			
Bored			
Disgusted			
Embarrassed			
Sorry			
Confused			
Surprised			
Concerned			
Total # Given _____ Total # Correct _____		% Correct _____	

Understanding Emotions

	Scenario 1	Scenario 2	Additional Scenarios
Set 1—Basic Emotions			
Happy			
Sad			
Angry			
Scared			
Neutral			

Total # Given _____ Total # Correct _____ | % Correct _____

	Scenario 1	Scenario 2	Additional Scenarios
Set 2—Intensity			
Very Happy			
A Little Happy			
Very Sad			
A Little Sad			
Very Angry			
A Little Angry			
Very Scared			
A Little Scared			

Total # Given _____ Total # Correct _____ | % Correct _____

	Scenario 1	Scenario 2	Additional Scenarios
Set 3—Other Emotions			
Interested			
Bored			
Disgusted			
Embarrassed			
Sorry			
Confused			
Surprised			
Concerned			

Total # Given _____ Total # Correct _____ | % Correct _____

Scenarios—Other Emotions for Assessment

Use these scenarios for assessment. Present in random order.

Interested

Choose 2 of the following scenarios, or more if needed.

You are watching a great movie that you really like.

▶ Show how your face would look. (Use with the Using Facial Expressions Assessment)

▶ Would you be feeling bored, interested or concerned? (Use with the Understanding Emotions Assessment)

You love talking with your friend about video games. Your friend is telling you about a new game.

▶ Show how your face would look.

▶ Would you be feeling interested, sorry or disgusted?

You are reading a great book.

▶ Show how your face would look.

▶ Would you be feeling confused, bored, or interested?

You like listening to the funny stories your teacher tells when he explains things.

▶ Show how your face would look.

▶ Would you be feeling sorry, sad or interested?

Your friend is about to tell you a big secret.

▶ Show how your face would look.

▶ Would you be feeling interested, bored, or confused?

Your parent is about to tell you where you're going on vacation.

▶ Show how your face would look.

▶ Would you be feeling doubtful, interested, or angry?

Not Interested or Bored

Choose 2 of the following scenarios, or more if needed.

There is a guest speaker talking to your class. He talks very quietly and you don't know what he's talking about.

▶ Show how your face would look.

▶ Would you be feeling surprised, bored or interested?

The kid who sits next to you is always talking about different kinds of boats. You really don't want to hear any more about boats.

▶ Show how your face would look.

▶ Would you be feeling not interested, concerned or doubtful?

For homework you have to copy all these sentences and write them correctly.

▶ Show how your face would look.

▶ Would you be feeling interested, bored or surprised?

You're cleaning your room.

▶ Show how your face would look.

▶ Would you be feeling concerned, interested or not interested?

You are waiting in a long line at the store.

▶ Show how your face would look.

▶ Would you be feeling bored, confused or interested?

You are riding in the car and it's taking forever to get where you're going.

▶ Show how your face would look.

▶ Would you be feeling disgusted, happy or bored?

Disgusted

Choose 2 of the following scenarios, or more if needed.

Someone just accidentally spit in your face when they were talking to you.

▶ Show how your face would look.

▶ Would you be feeling bored, concerned or disgusted?

The student sitting next to you just threw up on your shoe.

▶ Show how your face would look.

▶ Would you be feeling disgusted, sad or confused?

A little kid picks up old chewing gum from the ground and puts it in his mouth.

▶ Show how your face would look.

▶ Would you be feeling angry, disgusted or jealous?

Someone spit in the drinking fountain.

▶ Show how your face would look.

▶ Would you be feeling embarrassed, bored or disgusted?

You eat some food that has a long hair in it.

▶ Show how your face would look.

▶ Would you be feeling shy, disgusted or ashamed?

Your friend's dog licked you right on your mouth.

▶ Show how your face would look.

▶ Would you be feeling scared, sad or disgusted?

Embarrassed

Choose 2 of the following scenarios, or more if needed.

You came into the classroom after everyone was already there and tripped and fell while everyone was watching.

▶ Show how your face would look.

▶ Would you be feeling embarrassed, bored or doubtful?

While talking to your friend you accidentally spit in his face.

▶ Show how your face would look.

▶ Would you be feeling confident, jealous or embarrassed?

You burped right in the middle of your presentation in front of the class.

▶ Show how your face would look.

▶ Would you be feeling confident, jealous or embarrassed?

You messed up while you were playing a solo in front of others.

▶ Show how your face would look.

▶ Would you be feeling embarrassed, surprised or jealous?

You struck out each time you were up at bat.

▶ Show how your face would look.

▶ Would you be feeling confident, embarrassed or bored?

Right before class, the drinking fountain squirted water all over your pants.

▶ Show how your face would look.

▶ Would you be feeling happy, scared, or embarrassed?

Sorry or Ashamed

Choose 2 of the following scenarios, or more if needed.

The teacher caught you cheating while taking a test.

► Show how your face would look.

► Would you be feeling ashamed, jealous or bored?

Your friend caught you telling a secret that she had told you.

► Show how your face would look.

► Would you be feeling disgusted, bored or sorry?

You yelled at your friend, even though he didn't do anything wrong.

► Show how your face would look.

► Would you be feeling sorry, confused or jealous?

You took some money that wasn't yours and now you wish you hadn't.

► Show how your face would look.

► Would you be feeling ashamed, confident or bored?

You joined in with some kids who were bullying a new student, but you see how sad it made the new student feel.

► Show how your face would look.

► Would you be feeling happy, disgusted or ashamed?

Even though you didn't mean to, you said something that hurt your friend's feelings.

► Show how your face would look.

► Would you be feeling sorry, scared or confused?

Confused

Choose 2 of the following scenarios, or more if needed.

You're trying to do your homework, but you can't figure out what you're supposed to do.

▶ Show how your face would look.

▶ Would you be feeling confused, bored or surprised?

You forgot about the time change and arrived an hour early and can't figure out where everyone is.

▶ Show how your face would look.

▶ Would you be feeling jealous, confused or shy?

You don't understand what the teacher is trying to tell you.

▶ Show how your face would look.

▶ Would you be feeling surprised, sad or confused?

Your friend is trying to tell you what happened, but what she's saying isn't making any sense?

▶ Show how your face would look.

▶ Would you be feeling shy, confused or embarrassed?

You were sure you left your backpack on the kitchen table, but it's not there.

▶ Show how your face would look.

▶ Would you be feeling bored, scared or confused?

Your friend said your class project is due Thursday, but you were sure it wasn't due until Friday.

▶ Show how your face would look.

▶ Would you be feeling confused, sad or jealous?

Surprised

Choose 2 of the following scenarios, or more if needed.

You never expected to win the contest, but you did.

▶ Show how your face would look.

▶ Would you be feeling surprised, confused or bored?

You didn't know that your grandparents were coming for a visit, but when you got home, there they were.

▶ Show how your face would look.

▶ Would you be feeling jealous, disgusted or surprised?

Your teacher suddenly chose you to be the lead in a play.

▶ Show how your face would look.

▶ Would you be feeling sad, surprised or ashamed?

Your friend got up in front of everyone and sang a song. You never thought he would do that.

▶ Show how your face would look.

▶ Would you be feeling surprised, scared or confused?

When you got home you found out that you were going to an amusement park.

▶ Show how your face would look.

▶ Would you be feeling doubtful, concerned or surprised?

You received a present even though it wasn't your birthday.

▶ Show how your face would look.

▶ Would you be feeling concerned, surprised or disgusted?

Concerned

Choose 2 of the following scenarios, or more if needed.

Your friend is upset, but you don't know why.

▶ Show how your face would look.

▶ Would you be feeling disgusted, embarrassed or concerned?

Your mother is really sick.

▶ Show how your face would look.

▶ Would you be feeling angry, concerned or ashamed?

Someone has been sending mean notes to your best friend.

▶ Show how your face would look.

▶ Would you be feeling concerned, jealous or embarrassed?

Your friend has to give a report in front of the class and he's really nervous. He looks at you before he starts his report.

▶ Show how your face would look.

▶ Would you be feeling sick, confused or concerned?

Your pet is really sick.

▶ Show how your face would look.

▶ Would you be feeling concerned, ashamed or embarrassed?

You see a dog get hit by a car.

▶ Show how your face would look.

▶ Would you be feeling confused, scared or concerned?

Looking at People's Faces
Reminder Story

▶ People's faces are always changing.

▶ Faces can look lots of different ways.

▶ People's faces change depending on what they're feeling.

▶ When someone is feeling happy, his face will look happy.

▶ When someone is feeling sad, her face will look sad.

▶ It's important to look at people's faces and see how they are feeling.

▶ If I know how someone is feeling, I will have a better idea about what to do and say. I'm a kind person who usually tries to help others feel better.

▶ I know I can joke with someone who is feeling happy.

▶ I should be nice to someone who is feeling sad to help him feel better.

▶ I need to be careful when I see that someone is angry, so the person doesn't get more upset or mad at me.

▶ Sometimes I forget to look at people's faces and think about how they are feeling, but it's important to see how people are feeling.

▶ I will try to remember to _____

_____

_____

▶ Something I can do to help me remember is _____

_____

_____

When Somebody Is Talking to Me
Reminder Story

▶ People talk to each other all the time.

▶ When someone talks to another person, they like the other person to listen.

▶ When someone sees other people looking at him while he is talking, he knows that the other people are listening to him. That makes him feel good.

▶ When listeners are not looking at the speaker, the speaker thinks they are not listening. He thinks that they don't care about what he has to say. That makes the speaker feel sad or angry.

▶ Sometimes when people are talking to me, I don't look at them, even when I am listening to them.

▶ When a speaker sees me not looking, he thinks I'm not listening. He thinks I don't care about what he has to say. That can make him feel sad or angry. I am a kind person who doesn't like to make people feel bad.

▶ It's hard to always remember to look at a speaker's face, but it's important to do that.

▶ I will try to remember to _____

_____

_____

▶ Something I can do to help me remember is _____

_____

_____

Smiling Reminder Story

▶ When a person smiles at someone, she is being friendly. It's like she is inviting the other person to smile back or to say, "hello."

▶ When a person smiles at someone and that person doesn't smile or say anything, the smiling person thinks the other person doesn't like him or doesn't want to be friendly. That can make the smiling person feel sad or angry.

▶ When the other person smiles back and says something nice to the smiling person, everyone feels happier.

▶ Smiling is a way to tell others that you want to be friendly.

▶ I have a great smile and if I smile at other people, they will usually smile and be friendly to me.

▶ I can show others that I want to be friendly by smiling back when they smile at me.

▶ I like it when people are friendly to me, so I will try to remember to

_____

_____

_____

▶ Something I can do to help me remember is _____

_____

_____

UNIT 1
Recognizing Facial Expressions

Objectives for Unit 1

▶ Students will be able to recognize that different parts of the face change to create facial expressions

▶ Students will be able to match similar facial expressions

▶ Students will be able to recognize what the eyes and mouth look like for the following facial expressions; happy, sad, angry and scared

▶ Students will be able to label facial expressions as happy, sad, angry, scared or neutral

Teaching Activities

What Are Facial Expressions?

Get students attention by making a number of exaggerated facial expressions. An alternative way to start the lesson is to ask students to watch you and tell what you're doing, then make a number of exaggerated facial expressions. Make sure that you include expressions of happiness, sadness, fear and anger.

Explain to students that the different ways a face can look are called "facial expressions." Write the term "facial expressions" on the board.

Explain that people use facial expressions to tell you how they're feeling and what they're thinking and that facial expressions are often used instead of words to tell people things. If you can't tell what someone's face is saying, then you won't understand many of the messages that they are trying to tell you. Also, if your facial expressions don't match what you're thinking and feeling, other people won't get the messages about what's going on inside you.

Seeing the Differences

Describe how faces can change by demonstrating exaggerated expressions showing happiness, sadness, fear and anger. Cover parts of your face with a piece of poster board or paper and ask students to look at how the different parts of your face change as you demonstrate the following. (The point here is not to label the expressions, but to be aware of how different parts of the face change.)

▶ Mouth changes with a smile (happy), frown (sad), tightly closed or clenched teeth (angry) and open mouth, but not smiling (scared)

▶ Eyebrows change with surprise, frown, and questioning look

▶ Eyes wide open, downcast and squinting

▶ Face muscles tense and relax

Facial Expression Chart

Begin by creating a happy face chart and then a sad face chart, followed by several reinforcement activities—Mirror Practice, Sign Language and Taking Photos. Then repeat the chart making and reinforcement activities for an angry facial expression and then for a scared expression.

▶ Glue the **Happy Face** from **page 55** on a piece of chart paper. (Enlarge face if needed.)

▶ Ask students to tell you what emotion the face is showing. If necessary, tell students that this face looks happy.

▶ Tell students that you are going to study the face to figure out what makes this a happy face.

▶ Use a piece of poster board or paper to cover up the top part of the face, so that only the mouth is showing. Ask students to describe the mouth. (It's smiling, the corners are turned up.)

▶ Either write the description or draw a picture on the chart to illustrate a happy mouth. (See example below.)

▶ Next cover the lower part of the face with the poster board and describe the eyes, eyebrows, and cheeks.

▶ Write a description or draw a picture on the chart.

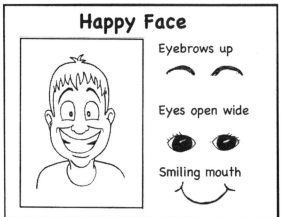

Help students understand that these are only general guidelines, that people may express the same emotion differently. As students work through these units, point out examples of how expressions look different on different people.

Sad Face Chart

▶ Repeat the steps above to create a sad face chart, noting that the corners of the eyes, eyebrows and mouth go down.

Matching Faces

▶ Make copies and cut out the **Facial Expression Cards** from **pages 57–66** ahead of time. Sort them into two groups: cartoons and realistic drawings. (These cards will be used for a variety of activities so mounting them on poster board and laminating them is recommended.) Have students take turns matching the Facial Expression Cards with the larger happy and sad face charts, beginning with the cartoons. Point out how the same emotion can look different on different people.

▶ You may also want to use pictures you collect from magazines or purchase commercially. (See resources in Introduction.)

Mirror Practice

▶ Have a student stand in front of a mirror. Have the student place one hand on each side of his or her face. To illustrate a happy face, tell the student to push up with both hands and for sad to push down. Have students practice making happy and sad faces, using their hands and without using their hands.

▶ Using hand mirrors, have students imitate happy and sad faces.

Guessing Game

▶ Start with the teacher making faces and have students guess if it's a happy or sad face. Then have students make happy or sad faces (checking their own face in the mirror if needed), having the teacher or other students guess. Again, point out how emotions may look slightly different on different people.

Treasure Hunt

▶ Have students search through old magazines, comics or greeting cards to find happy and sad faces. (Save these pictures for the picture sort and facial expression collages. See below.)

Picture Sort

▶ Have students sort happy and sad faces that have been cut from a magazine or other source. (Use pictures that students collected from their treasure hunt.)

Facial Expression Collage

▶ Using pictures from magazines, have students make happy/sad posters or collages.

Taking Photos

▶ Take digital photos of students trying to look happy and sad. Display the photos on the computer and ask students to evaluate if the facial expression displays what the student was trying to express.

Happy, Sad and Neutral Faces

▶ Repeat the steps listed above under **Facial Expression Chart,** using the **Neutral Face** from **page 56** to create a neutral face chart.

► Repeat some or all of the activities above, as needed to ensure mastery (Matching Faces, Mirror Practice, Guessing Game, Treasure Hunt, Picture Sort, Facial Expression Collage and Taking Photos) using happy, sad and neutral facial expressions.

Happy, Sad, Neutral and Angry Faces

► Repeat the steps listed above, using the **Angry Face** from **page 55**. Repeat reinforcement activities as needed using happy, sad, neutral and angry facial expressions.

Happy, Sad, Neutral, Angry and Scared Faces

► Repeat the steps listed above, using the **Scared Face** from **page 56**. Repeat reinforcement activities as needed using happy, sad, neutral, angry and scared facial expressions.

Fun and Games: Additional Learning Activities

Mirror Image

► Have students practice making facial expressions with their mirrors again. Then pair up students and have one student in each pair hold up an imaginary mirror while the other student faces student #1. As student number #1 makes a facial expression, student #2 tries to be the mirror image by imitating each expression. Have students reverse roles.

Sign Language

► Learning sign language for these basic emotions can be useful since these hand signs duplicate and emphasize the facial expression to a certain degree. Either distribute or display copies of the signs on page 67. Demonstrate the sign for happy and sad. Have students note how the happy sign indicates a lifting, moving up motion and the sad indicates a sinking, moving down one. Have students practice these signs. Repeat with the signs for angry, noting the tension in the hand and how everything is being pulled to the center of the face. Repeat again with the sign for scared, again noticing the tension in the hands and how the hands extend and spread out, the same as the face does when someone is frightened. Finally, note the calm, relaxed feeling for the neutral sign. (This is actually the sign for "rest" or "restful.") Have students practice all of these signs and use them when talking about these feelings during other activities.

Candid Camera

▶ Take photos of students as they go through their daily activities. At a later time, look over the photos, either individually or in a group, and describe the facial expressions they exhibit.

Sunday Funnies

▶ Make copies of cartoons and comic strips and place them on the overhead. Have students label the facial expressions. Use one of the following comic strips or other personal favorites. Archives of comics can usually be found on the comic strip's website.

• Peanuts — **http://www.unitedmedia.com/comics/peanuts**

• Stan 'n' Isaac — **http://www.stan-isaac.com**

• Calvin and Hobbes — **http://ucomics.com**

• Garfield — **http://garfield.com**

• Grand Avenue — **http://www.comics.com**

• Luann — **http://www.luannsroom.com**

• Zits — **http://www.kingfeatures.com**

Stop Action

▶ Play short segments of DVDs or videos with the sound turned off. Hit pause and have students label the facial expression.

Charades—Basic Emotions

▶ Make a copy of the **Facial Expression Word Cards** from **page 44,** cut them up and if desired mount them on lightweight poster board. Place the cards in a bag or box or place them face down. Each student draws a card and without letting anyone see the card, displays the facial expression written on the card, while other students attempt to guess. Have facial expression charts available for all students to refer to if necessary. (This is a good opportunity to take photos of students' facial expressions to use in other activities.)

▶ To make a competitive game, divide students into teams having teammates attempting to guess the facial expressions of other teammates while you keep track of how long it takes for the team to guess the correct answer. The team with the least total guessing time wins.

Facial Expression Simon Says

▶ Play Simon Says using facial expressions, such as, "Simon Says look happy."

Matching Expressions Lotto

Facial Expression Lotto

▶ Make copies of the **Lotto Card Game** from **page 43** and copy some of the **Facial Expression Cards** from **pages 57–66**. Choose cartoons or drawings or a combination of both, depending on students' abilities. Create a variety of lotto cards by copying and gluing the Facial Expression Cards onto the spaces on the lotto cards, making each card different.

▶ Use the Facial Expression Cards created for the Matching Faces activities. Place the cards face down in a pile. Have a student draw a card. Then either have the student who drew the card place it on a matching facial expression on his or her lotto card (a happy face on top of another happy face) or have each student place a marker on the matching expression on each of their cards.

Labeling Lotto

Facial Expression Lotto

neutral ☺	happy ☺	sad ☹
angry ☹	Free	scared 😨
sad ☹	angry ☹	happy ☺

▶ Make multiple copies of the **Lotto Game Card** from **page 43** and glue each one on a piece of poster board. Make multiple copies of the facial expression word cards from page 44, cut them out and glue them onto the squares on the lotto game cards, placing them in random order, so that each card is different. See example below. You may want to laminate the lotto cards to make them more durable.

▶ Place the **Facial Expression Cards (pages 57–66)** face down or in a container. Either draw and show a card to students or have students take turns drawing the cards. After each card is drawn, students place a marker on the corresponding facial expression square on their lotto board.

A Book With a Mirror

▶ A great resource for young preschoolers and primary age students is the book, *Make a Face: A Book with a Mirror* by Henry & Amy Schwartz (Scholastic: Cartwheel Books, 1994). Each page presents a different facial expression, with a mirror that can be folded down for the child to use to practice making the expression shown.

A Mirror Book for Older Students

▶ The idea can be replicated for older students by creating a book using a notebook binder and pictures from magazines, photos of students or clip-art. (See example on page 41.) Mount a sheet of Silver Mirror Board inside the back cover of the binder. (Silver Mirror Board is available through art and craft suppliers.)

Books and Mirrors

▶ Use some of the books below, looking at the pictures and labeling the facial expressions. A mirror can also be used for the students to imitate the expressions. Illustrations from the books listed in **Unit 2 —Understanding Emotions (pages 69–71)** could also be used.

- Elffers, J. (1999). *How Are You Peeling?* New York: Arthur A. Levine Books.
- Lalli, J. (1991). *Feelings Alphabet: An Album of Emotions from A to Z.* Austin, TX: Jalmar Press
- Rotner, S. (2003). *Lots of Feelings.* Brookfield, CT: The Millbrook Press, Inc.

Cross Curricular Activities

Art—Make a Flip Book

▶ Make copies of the **Face Outline** on **page 45** in the resource section. Make enough copies so each student has five sheets. Lightweight tag board could be used instead of paper to make the book more durable.

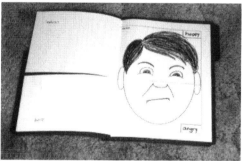

▶ Have students write the feeling words (happy, sad, angry, scared, and neutral) in the boxes at the top and the bottom of each page.

▶ Students then draw eyes, eyebrows and a mouth to show each emotion. Students may then color in the pictures, adding hair, hats or other details.

▶ Have students fold an 11 x 17 inch piece of paper in half to make a cover and place the 5 completed face outlines inside. Staple along the left side to secure the pages.

▶ Finally, have students cut along the dotted line on each sheet and look at the funny faces that result when the eyes don't match the mouth.

Art Appreciation

▶ Introduce students to famous works of art, by examining different facial expressions in paintings. Norman Rockwell paintings provide extensive examples and are easily available in books or calendars. The following are books written for elementary age students that look at faces in famous artwork.

- Baumbusch, B. (1999). *The Many Faces of the Face.* New York: Stewart, Tabori & Chang.
- Delafosse, C. (1995). *Portraits (A First Discovery Art Book).* New York: Scholastic.
- Richardson, J. (2000). *Looking at Faces in Art (How to Look at Art series).* Milwaukee, WI: Gareth Stevens Publishing.

Art—Cartooning and Drawing

▶ Teaching students how to draw cartoons can be a fun way for them to learn about facial expressions. Use the following resources to help students learn how to draw facial expressions.

   • Artel, M. (2001). *Cartooning for Kids.* New York: Sterling Publishing Company, Inc.

   • Gamble, K. (1997). *You Can Draw Amazing Faces.* New York: KD Publishing, Inc.

   • Mayne, D. (2000). *Draw Your Own Cartoons!* Charlotte, VT: Williamson Publishing Co.

   • Ozawa, T. (2001). *How to Draw Anime & Game Characters, Vol. 2: Expressing Emotions. Japan: Graphic-Sha.* (Also available in Spanish.)

Independent Reinforcement Activities

Activity Pages

▶ Make copies of the **Activity pages 46–53** and have students complete.

Folder Tasks and Work Systems

Reinforcement activities can be provided in a structured learning format by creating matching and sorting work systems or folder tasks. (See Introduction for further information.) Use the following examples or create your own.

▶ Match pictures of similar types of facial expressions, using cartoons, drawings or photos

▶ Match pictures of similar types of facial expressions, mixing cartoons, drawings and photos

▶ Sort pictures into categories of different types of facial expressions (happy, sad, angry, scared, and neutral) using cartoons, drawings or photos

▶ Match pictures of facial expressions with the corresponding word

Facial Expression Lotto

	Free	

Facial Expression Word Cards

neutral	happy	happy
sad	sad	angry
angry	scared	scared

Flip Book Template

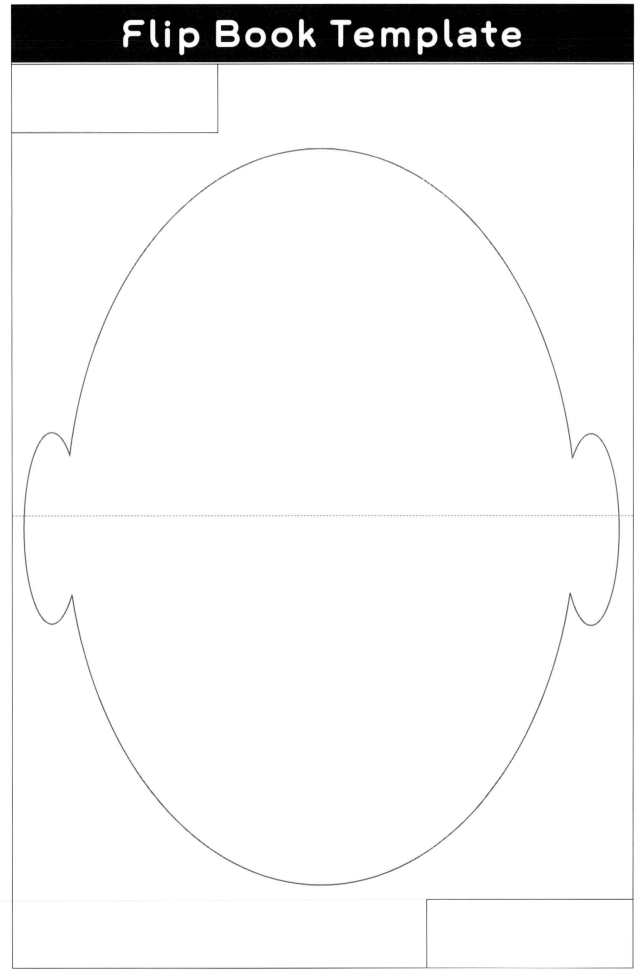

Which face is different?

Circle the face in each row that shows a different emotion than the other two.

Which face is different?

Circle the face in each row that shows a different emotion than the other two.

Match the faces

Draw a line from each face on the left to the face on the right with the same type of facial expression.

Name _____

Match the faces

Cut out the faces on the right. Glue each one next to the matching facial expression on the left.

 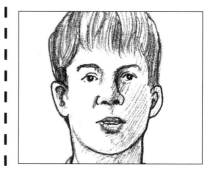

Match the words and faces

Draw a line from each word on the left to the matching face on the right.

| happy | 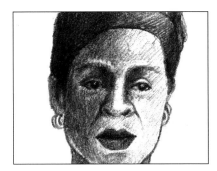 |

| sad |  |

| angry |  |

| scared |  |

| neutral |  |

Name_____

Name that facial expression

Write the word from the Word Bank that describes each facial expression.

Word Bank
happy   angry   neutral   sad   scared

Drawing faces

Draw mouths to complete the facial expression.

Draw eyes and eyebrows to complete the facial expression.

Drawing faces

Draw mouths, eyes, and eyebrows to make the following faces.

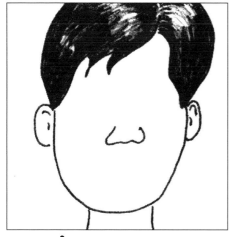
happy

sad

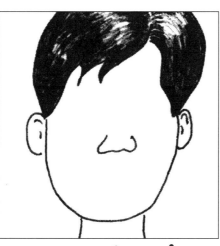
neutral

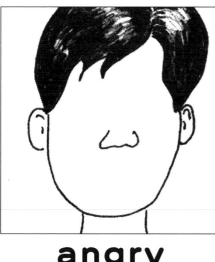
angry

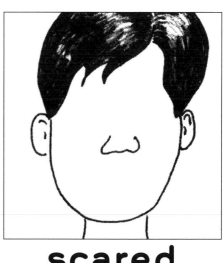
scared

Teaching Faces

Happy

Sad

Angry

Scared

Neutral

Blank

Drawings—Happy Faces

Cartoons—Scared Faces

happy

neutral

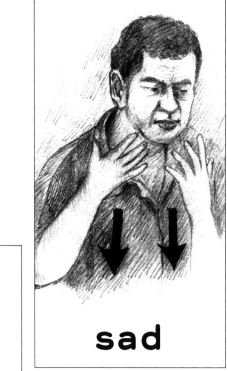

sad

angry

scared

UNIT 2
Understanding Emotions

Objectives for Unit 2

▶ Students will recognize that emotions change depending on what is happening

▶ Students will identify how their body responds to certain emotions

▶ Students will be able to identify certain emotions with certain events

Teaching Activities

How Does That Make You Feel?

Copy and cut out the **Emotion Picture Cards** on **pages 97– 101**. Write the basic feeling words (happy, sad, angry, scared and neutral) on a board, leaving space between them. A student will then draw one of the Emotion Picture Cards, tell how the card makes her feel and place it under or next to that feeling word. (See illustration at right.) You may also want to use photographs collected from magazines or commercially available photo cards depicting various events.

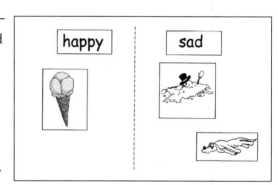

Read About Emotions

Read aloud books describing the four basic emotions, choosing from the suggested books below or others. Ask students to describe times when they have felt happy, sad, angry or scared.

▶ Books Describing Different Emotions

• Feeney, K. (2002). *Feel Good: Understand Your Emotions*. Mankato, MN: Capstone Press. (primary)

▶ Feeling Happy

• Barclay, J. (2002). *Going on a Journey to the Sea*. Montreal, Quebec: Lobster Press. (primary)

• Bertrand, D. (2004). *My Pal Victor*. Green Bay, WI: Raven Tree Press. (primary – with text in English and Spanish)

• Joosse, B. (1995). *Snow Day!* New York: Clarion Books. (primary)

• Wilcox, B. (2001). *Hip, Hip Hooray for Annie McRae!* Salt Lake City, UT: Gibbs Smith, Publisher. (primary)

- Budd, E. (2000). *Thoughts and Feelings: Glad.* Chanhassen, MN: The Child's World, Inc. (primary – intermediate)

- Rylant, C. (1985). *The Relatives Came.* New York: Simon & Schuster. (primary-intermediate)

- Wood, D. (2005). *The Secret of Saying Thanks.* New York: Simon & Schuster. (intermediate)

▶ Feeling Sad

- Berry, J. (1996). *Let's Talk about Feeling Sad.* New York: Scholastic Inc. (primary)

- Harper, J. (2004). *I Like Where I Am.* New York: G.P. Putnam's Sons. (primary)

- Spelman, C. (2002). *When I Feel Sad.* Morton Grove, IL: Albert Whitman. (primary)

- Tester, S. (2000). *Sad.* Chanhassen, MN: The Child's World, Inc. (primary)

- Viorst, J. (1972). *Alexander and the Terrible, Horrible, No Good, Very Bad Day.* New York: Aladdin Paperbacks. (primary)

- Danneberg, J. (2006). *Last Day Blues.* Watertown, MA: Charlesbridge. (primary – intermediate)

- Bunting, E. (2001). *The Days of Summer.* Orlando, FL: Harcourt, Inc. (intermediate)

- Bunting, E. (1990). *The Wall.* New York: Clarion Books. (intermediate)

- Rosen, M. (2004). *Michael Rosen's Sad Book.* Cambridge, MA: Candlewick Press. (intermediate)

▶ Feeling Angry

- Bang, M. (1999). *When Sophie Gets Angry – Really, Really Angry.* New York: The Blue Sky Press. (primary)

- Berry, J. (1996) *Let's Talk About Feeling Angry.* New York: Scholastic, Inc. (primary)

- Kroll, S. (2002) *That Makes Me Mad.* New York: SeaStar Books. (primary)

- Riley, S. (1998). *Angry.* Chanhassen, MN: Child's World, Inc. (primary)

- Althea, (2001). *Choices: Feeling Angry.* London: A&C Black Ltd. (primary – intermediate)

- Fox, L. (2000). *I Am So Angry I Could Scream: Helping Children Deal with Anger.* Far Hills, NJ: New Horizon Press. (primary – intermediate)

- Johnston, T. (2001). *Uncle Rain Cloud.* Watertown, MA: Charlesbridge Publishing. (intermediate)

▶ Feeling Scared

- Berry, J. (1995). *Let's Talk About Feeling Afraid.* New York: Scholastic, Inc. (primary)

- Riley, S. (2000). *Afraid.* Chanhassen, MN: The Child's World. (primary)

- Spelman, C. (2002) *When I Feel Scared.* Morton Grove, IL: Albert Whitman & Co. (primary)

- Althea. (2002). *Choices: Feeling Scared.* London: A&C Black Ltd. (primary – intermediate)

- London, J. (1998). *Hurricane.* New York: Lothrop, Lee & Shepard Books. (primary – intermediate)

- Polacco, P. (1991). *Some Birthday.* New York: Simon & Schuster books for Young Readers. (primary – intermediate)

- Powling, C. (2002). *The Kingfisher Book of Scary Stories.* New York: Kingfisher. (intermediate)

What Does It Feel Like? Chart

Ask students to describe how their body feels when they experience the four basic emotions — happy, sad, angry and scared. Write their responses on chart paper. Use the items on the lists below if needed. Save the lists to refer to.

▶ Happy

- Lots of energy — feel like running and jumping
- I like everyone
- Feel like smiling and laughing
- Everything seems fun

▶ Sad

- Nothing seems fun
- Don't want to do anything
- Feel like crying
- Feel all alone

▶ Angry

- Feel like a pot of boiling water about ready to explode
- Want to yell or hit or hurt others
- Feel that things aren't fair
- Feel like people are mean

▶ Scared

- Want to run and hide
- Hands sweat
- Heart beats really fast
- Stomach hurts

What Makes Me Feel...

On the top of a sheet of paper, have students write, "Things that make me feel happy," then list five or more things that make them happy. Younger students or students who have difficulty writing could draw pictures or cut and glue pictures on the page. Repeat with sad, angry, and scared.

Feelings Check In

Set aside a few minutes each day to have students relate how they are feeling. Use visuals, such as a chart if needed. Have feeling words available for students to refer to, or use pictures or expression icons. Ask students to describe what they're feeling and explain why they think they are feeling that way. Older students could relate their feelings in a journal. Students who have difficulty writing could draw or circle a face that shows how he is feeling and perhaps draw a picture that illustrates why he feels that way.

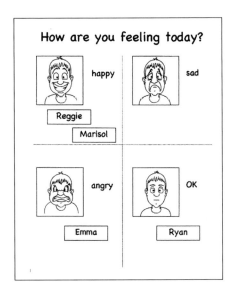

Read and Pause

Read aloud a book that expresses a variety of the basic emotions. (See suggested books listed below.) After each emotional event, stop reading and ask students what the character is likely feeling and have them demonstrate how the character's face probably would look.

▶ Layton, N. (2001). *The Sunday Blues.* Cambridge, MA: Candlewick Press. (primary)

▶ Stadler, A. (2003). *Lila Bloom.* New York: Farrar, Straus & Giroux. (primary)

▶ Stanek, M. (1985). *All Alone After School.* Niles, IL: Albert Whitman & Company. (primary)

▶ dePaola, T. (1973). *Nana Upstairs, Nana Downstairs.* New York: G.P. Putnam's Sons. (primary–intermediate)

▶ Bunting, E. (1994). *A Day's Work.* New York: Clarion books. (intermediate)

▶ Bunting, E. (1991). *Fly Away Home.* New York: Clarion Books. (intermediate)

▶ Polacco, P. (1992). *Chicken Sunday.* New York: Philomel Books. (intermediate)

▶ Van Allsburg, C. (1981). *Jumanji.* New York: Houghton Mifflin Co. (intermediate)

Dictionary of Emotions

Provide copies of the basic facial expressions from this curriculum or have students find other pictures. Have students place one picture on each page, write the word that matches the expression and have students write a description or draw (or cut and paste) a picture of a situation when someone would feel that way. Place inside a binder for students to add to as they learn about other emotions. If appropriate, have students place the pages in alphabetical order.

Show How You Feel

Copy and cut out the **Show How You Feel Scenarios** on **page 78** and put the scenario strips in a box or bag. Have students take turns drawing and reading a scenario then displaying the appropriate facial expression. Other students watch and tell which emotion is being displayed.

Act and Pause

Make copies and cut apart the **Role-Plays on page 79**. Ask for volunteers to act out the role-plays. At the end of each short role-play have the actors pause, while the other students tell how they think the characters would be feeling.

What Do You Think Happened?

This activity requires some creative thinking and may not be appropriate for all students. Using some of the **Facial Expression Cards** from **pages 57–66**, have students take turns drawing a card, telling how the person is feeling and making up a brief scenario which would describe why she might be feeling that way. For example, the student draws a sad face and says that the person is sad because she's sick and unable to go to the school party.

Fun and Games: Additional Learning Activities

Draw a Face

Copy and distribute copies of **Drawing Faces — Part I and II, pages 89–90**. Read the statements below and have students draw the appropriate facial expression to match each statement. Remind students that they may draw neutral faces as well.

1. Her friend just told her a really funny joke.

2. A bully just threatened her.

3. She's riding in the car.

4. She lost the money she'd been saving up.

5. Someone cut in front of her in line.

6. He's reading during silent reading time.

7. He's on his way to the carnival.

8. He's lost and it's getting dark.

9. He's got the flu and is missing his best friend's birthday party.

10. A big kid deliberately tripped him.

Sunday Funnies

Using easily understood comic strips (see suggested **Sunday Funnies** on **page 39**), make transparencies and discuss what is happening in the comic, what the characters are feeling and their facial expressions.

Dice Game

Have students write the five basic feeling words on a piece of paper or on cards, one word on each card. Have students number each word as in the example below. Divide students into small groups, giving each group a die. Students take turns rolling the die and telling about a time he felt happy, sad, angry, scared or neutral, depending on the number rolled. After the student answers, then he can cross out that emotion word or turn over the card. Whoever crosses out all the emotion words first, or turns over all of his cards wins.

1. Happy   2. Sad   3. Angry   4. Scared   5. Neutral   6. Choose any one feeling word that remains

Emotions Lotto

Create a lotto board as directed under **Labeling Lotto** on **page 40**. Read short scenarios from **Scenarios—Basic Emotions, pages 80–82** or make up your own. Have students place a marker on the correct lotto square. There may be some variation in how students view a particular scenario. For example, the same scenario could be viewed as sad by some, while it would make others angry.

Name That Emotion

Have several "contestants" compete at a time. Read a short scenario from pages 80–82 and have students raise their hands to name the emotion. First hand up gets to answer. Keep score and the first person to score five wins.

Movie Time

Watch a movie with lots of emotional ups and downs and pause and discuss what the characters are feeling.

Cross Curricular Activities

Communication Skills

Pair up students and have them take turns interviewing each other, using the **Interview Sheet** on **page 91** to write down the other's responses. When completed, have each interviewer relate to the interviewee what she understood him to say, with the interviewee pointing out any misunderstandings.

Read Aloud

During daily read aloud times, pause and discuss the character's feelings at emotional highpoints of the story. Have students draw pictures of the characters' faces to show their facial expressions.

Reading—Find the Feeling

Before students begin reading, provide them with a list of the four basic feeling words (happy, sad, angry and scared) and a copy of the **Emotions in Stories Sheet, page 92**. Have students write down the characters' names and page numbers when different emotions were expressed in the story.

Reading and Graphic Organizers

Make copies and distribute the **Story Organizer** on **page 93** or provide one appropriate to student's level. As students complete their reading, have them fill in what happened and what the characters felt.

Act It Out

Incorporate a little drama as part of your reading program by having students act out stories or parts of stories that they have read or use short plays written at the appropriate reading level. Discuss how the character would feel and emphasize using appropriate facial expressions.

Write About It

Incorporate emotions into your creative writing program, using some of the following ideas. Have students write about the following:

▶ Times when they felt happy, sad, angry or scared

▶ Things that make them feel happy, sad, angry or scared

▶ How they felt when...(first day of school, school was closed for a snow day, the class hamster died, etc.)

▶ Make up a scary story

▶ Write their own version of *Alexander and the Terrible, Horrible, No Good, Very Bad Day* (Viorst, J. 1972)

▶ Write a sad story, with a happy ending

Following Directions

Copy and hand out directions and sheets for making a **"Changing Emotions Face," pages 83–87**. Use stiff paper or cardstock for pages 84–87. Have a completed model available to students to see. Have students read and complete directions, providing assistance as needed. With younger students, it may be necessary to cut out the mouth and eyeholes ahead of time. The feeling words could be written on the wheels ahead of time for students who have difficulty with handwriting.

Art with Feeling

Have students draw, paint or create collages depicting different emotions.

Art Appreciation

Examine famous works of art, as described in **Unit 1, page 41,** but add discussion about what they think is happening in the picture which causes the person or people to feel as they do. Norman Rockwell paintings not only have very expressive faces, but also provide a great deal of information about what is causing those facial expressions.

Art—Cartooning and Drawing

Take cartooning a step farther in this unit by having students draw a scene which explains why the cartoon character is feeling the way he does.

Independent Reinforcement Activities

Activity Sheets

Make copies of the **Activity Sheets, page 94–96** and have students complete.

Folder Tasks and Work Systems

The following matching and sorting tasks can be used in work systems or folder tasks.

▶ Match a scenario with a facial expression

▶ Match a written statement or description with a facial expression, such as "I can't believe I won first prize!" and "I'm home alone and the lights went out."

One of your friends is moving far away.

You got invited to a really fun party.

You hear a loud crashing noise in the middle of the night.

Your friend won't let you play his new video game.

You just found out you get to go on a really fun vacation.

Your parents won't let you go to see a movie you want to see.

Someone stole your money.

Your dog was hit by a car.

The car you're in starts sliding off the road.

Someone called you a name.

You made up with your friend after having a big fight.

Your dad can't take you swimming because he's sick.

It's the school picnic today. No work!

You wake up from a really bad dream.

Some kids won't let you play ball with them.

3–5 actors | Several students standing in line and another student cuts in.

2 actors | Two friends see each other after one has been gone all summer.

2 actors | A teacher sees a student cheating on a test.

2 actors | One kid grabs a video game controller while the other kid is playing with it.

3–4 actors | A parent tells kids that they are going to the carnival.

2 actors | Two kids are home alone at night when all the lights go out.

2 actors | One kid tells another kid that he/she doesn't want to play with him/her.

3 actors | The teacher just gave back a test. One student got an A+ and the other student got a D.

3–5 actors | The teacher surprised everyone with ice cream.

2 actors | Two kids are walking home and a big mean looking dog starts following them.

2 actors | One kid is reading and the other sneaks up behind him and then shouts.

Happy

▶ You just played a game and won.

▶ It's a snow day. No school!

▶ You just watched a really funny movie.

▶ You're having pizza (or your favorite food) for dinner.

▶ You got just what you wanted for your birthday.

▶ Your friend just told you a really funny joke.

▶ You're going shopping for some new clothes.

▶ Someone you really like just asked you to go to the movies.

▶ No work today at school. You're going on a fieldtrip!

▶ You're spending the day with your best friend.

Sad

▶ Your pet died.

▶ Your best friend is moving away.

▶ You got sick and missed the fieldtrip.

▶ Your friend doesn't want to hang out with you.

▶ Your friend is sick and had to cancel his/her party.

▶ Your team just lost the big game.

▶ Your best friend is away on vacation and you really miss him/her.

▶ You really wanted to be in the school play, but you weren't chosen.

▶ Your pet dog is very sick.

▶ You want to go swimming but you have a really bad cold.

Angry

▶ Your CD player won't work.

▶ Your teacher blamed you for something you didn't do.

▶ You can't watch your favorite TV show because your homework isn't finished.

▶ You really, really want a new jacket (video game, CD, etc.) but your parents said, "no."

▶ You're playing a game and the other team cheated.

▶ Another student deliberately tripped you.

▶ Someone you thought was your friend told on you and got you in trouble.

▶ You're trying to watch your favorite TV show, but everyone keeps talking really loud.

▶ Someone called you a name.

▶ Your parent promised to take you to the movie, but then said he/she couldn't.

Scared

▶ You hear strange noises in the middle of the night.

▶ You just had a really bad dream.

- You're lost and don't know how to get home.

- Your mother is sick and had to go to the hospital.

- You just watched a really good horror movie.

- You're riding on a really big roller coaster.

- There's a mean looking dog growling at you.

- You're walking in the woods and see a snake. You think it might be a poisonous snake.

- Your parents' car breaks down late at night and there's no one around.

- You hear a loud crashing noise coming from the next room.

Neutral

- You're riding in a car.

- You're getting ready for bed.

- You're eating breakfast.

- It's a typical Tuesday.

- You're watching some TV show. It's OK.

- It's cloudy outside for recess, but at least it's not raining.

- You collect the papers for your group.

- You bring in the mail.

- You feed the cat.

- You take your vitamin.

Making a Changing Emotions Face

1. Cut out the 'face card' along the dotted lines and cut out the mouth and eye holes.

2. Use a brad to poke a hole as shown.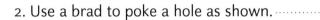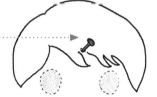

3. Cut out the 'eyes and eyebrows wheel' on page 86.

4. Draw 1 eye and 1 eyebrow in each oval.

5. Place the wheel behind the face so that the eyes and eyebrows show in the eye holes.

6. Use the brad to poke a hole in the wheel and fold the brad to hold the wheel in place.

7. Write the feeling words in the spaces at the top of the 'face card.

8. Cut out the 'back of head card' along the dotted lines.

9. Use a brad to poke a hole as shown.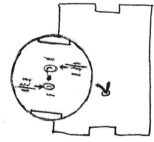

10. Cut out the 'mouth wheel' on page 87.

11. Draw a mouth in each oval.

12. Place the wheel to the blank side of the 'back of head card.'

13. Use the brad to poke a hole in the wheel and fold the brad to hold the wheel in place.

14. Write the feeling words in the spaces at the bottom of the 'face card.'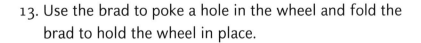

15. Tape the 'face card' and the 'back of the head card' together along both sides.

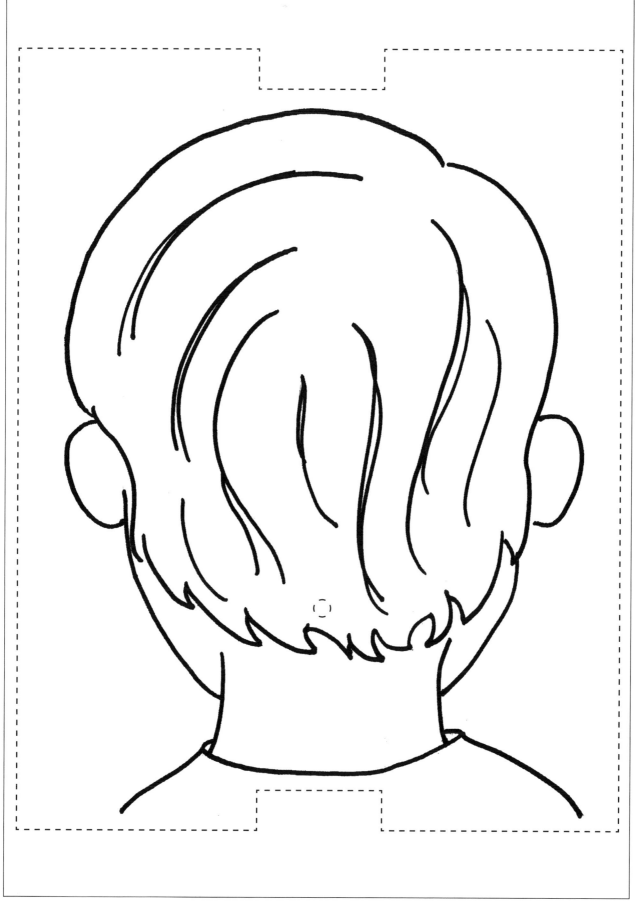

Eyes and Eyebrows Wheel

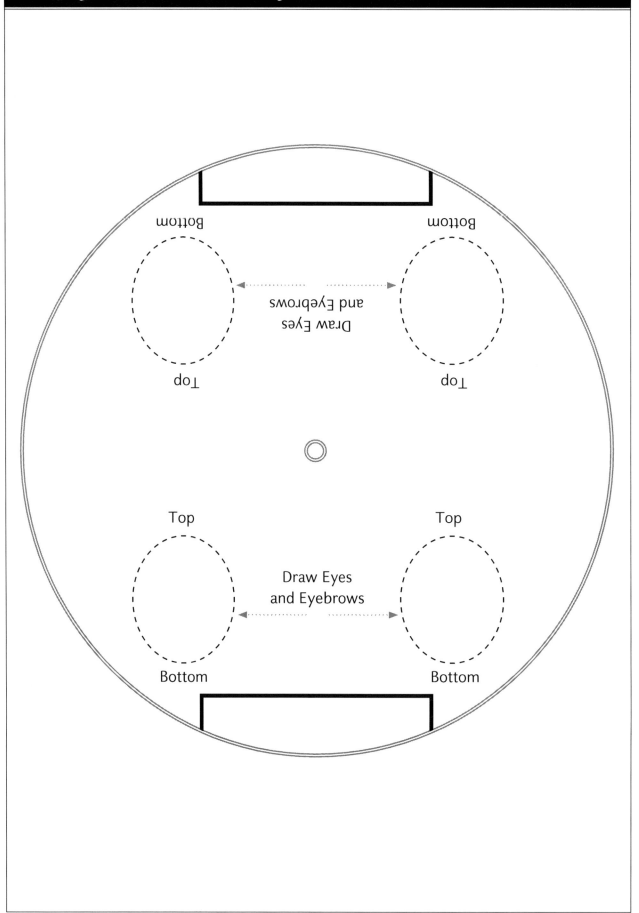

Draw Eyes and Eyebrows

Mouth Wheel

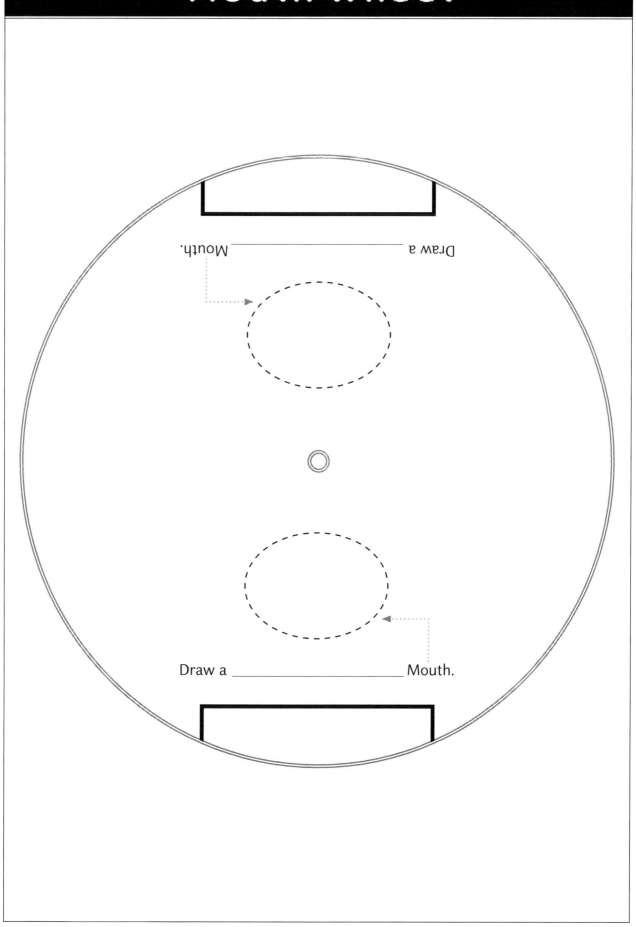

Draw a _____ Mouth.

Draw a _____ Mouth.

Drawing Faces—Part I

Draw mouths, eyes, and eyebrows to make the correct facial expression.

1.

2.

3.

4.

5.

Drawing Faces—Part II

Draw mouths, eyes, and eyebrows to make the correct facial expression.

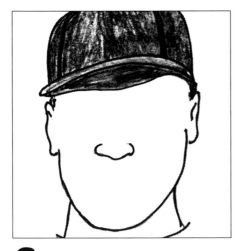

6.

7.

8.

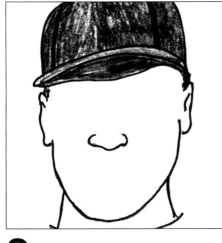

9.

10.

Name_____

Interview Sheet

Ask your partner the following questions and write what he or she tells you.

1. Tell about a time you felt happy.

_____

_____

_____

_____

2. Tell about a time you felt sad.

_____

_____

_____

_____

3. Tell 3 things that make you angry.

_____

_____

_____

4. Tell 3 things that make you feel scared.

_____

_____

_____

Emotions in Stories

The story is _____

Tell who feels happy, sad, angry or scared and write the page number.

The emotion	Who feels it	What page
_____	_____	_____
_____	_____	_____
_____	_____	_____
_____	_____	_____
_____	_____	_____
_____	_____	_____
_____	_____	_____
_____	_____	_____

Story Organizer

Name of story _____

Characters in story _____

_____

_____

What happened first?

How did the characters feel?

Then what happened?

How did the characters feel?

How did the story end?

How did the characters feel?

What are you feeling?

Use the words from the Word Bank to tell how you would feel.

1. It's your first day at a new school. _____

2. You are getting ready to go on vacation. _____

3. Someone called you a bad name. _____

4. A mean looking dog is growling at you. _____

5. Your team just won the game. _____

6. It's time to eat dinner. _____

7. Your friends went to a movie without you. _____

8. You're sick and can't go trick-or-treating. _____

9. You're riding home on the bus. _____

10. You are blamed for something you didn't do. _____

Word Bank
happy   angry   neutral   sad   scared

What are they thinking?

Draw a line from the face to the matching thought.

"It looks like a nice day out."

"I miss my friends so much."

"That dog looks really mean and he's heading right for me."

"That is just not fair!"

"This party is so much fun!"

Drawing Faces

Draw the face to show how the person is feeling.

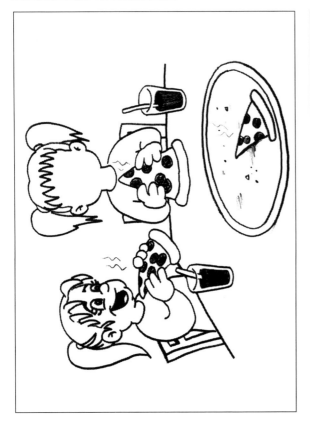

Getting the Message: Learning to Read Facial Expressions | **Activity Sheet** |

Happy Pictures

Angry Pictures

Scared Pictures

Getting the Message: Learning to Read Facial Expressions | **Emotion Pictures** |

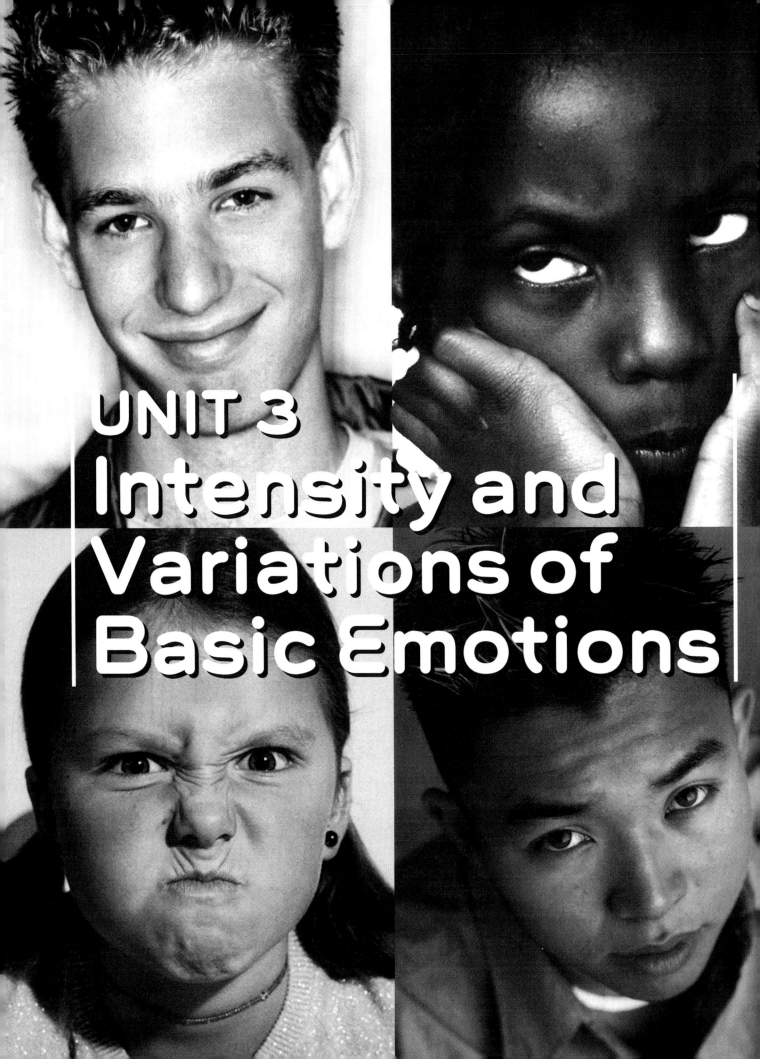

UNIT 3
Intensity and Variations of Basic Emotions

Objectives for Unit 3

- ► Students will discriminate between facial expressions which show intense and moderate emotions

- ► Students will label facial expressions which show different intensities of the basic emotions

- ► Students will identify different emotional intensities with different events

Teaching Activities

Recognizing Different Intensities of Feelings

Tell students that you are going to read different scenarios and ask them to tell you how each scenario would make them feel. Read the following scenarios or create your own.

- ► You just found out that you are having something good to eat for dinner.
- ► You just won a free trip to Disneyland.
- ► You're having a party this afternoon at school.
- ► You got a good grade on a report you did.

Ask if they would feel just the same in each scenario. Discuss how sometimes people feel a little happy, sometimes more happy, and sometimes very happy. Have students give their own examples of times they have felt different intensities of emotions.

3-Point Scale — Happy

Tell students that you are going to set up a three-point scale, with #1 being a little bit happy, #2 is happy, and #3 is very happy. Choose a word that would describe feeling a little bit happy, such as glad, pleased or content and a word to describe feeling really happy, such as great, terrific, excited or ecstatic. Choose words that are in line with the students' receptive vocabulary. (Refer to the **List of Feeling Words** on **page 115**.) If other words are too difficult, use the terms, "a little happy" and "very happy." Write these words on cards or on a large sheet of paper and post them on the board.

Read the **Intensity Scenarios—Happy** from **page 111** and have students tell you how it would make them feel on the 3-point scale. Or copy and cut out the scenarios and have students read them and place them into envelopes, as shown above.

Recognizing Intensity in Facial Expressions

Copy and cut out the **Facial Expression Cards—Emotional Intensity, pages 120–127**. Have students sort the happy facial expressions according to the 3-point scale (#1 pleased, #2 happy or #3 terrific), placing the pictures by the word or in envelopes.

Mirror Practice — Happy Faces

Using a mirror, have students practice making different intensity happy faces.

3-Point Scale — Sad

Tell students that you are now going to set up a 3-point scale for sad. Choose a word that describes feeling a little sad, such as feeling down, troubled, blue or unhappy and a word for feeling very sad, such as depressed, miserable, desolate or if these words are too difficult for the students, use the term "very sad."

Read the **Intensity Scenarios—Sad** on **page 112** and have students sort them.

Recognizing Intensity in Facial Expressions

Have students sort the **Sad Facial Expression Cards** from **page 122–123** according to the 3-point scale.

Mirror Practice — Sad Faces

Using a mirror, have students practice making different intensity sad faces.

3-Point Scale — Angry

Repeat the steps above creating a 3-point scale for angry. Use a word such as bothered, annoyed or upset to describe feeling a little angry. Use a word such as furious, enraged, fuming or really mad to describe feeling very angry.

Read the **Intensity Scenarios—Angry** on **page 113** and have students sort them.

Recognizing Intensity in Facial Expressions

Have students sort the **Angry Facial Expression Cards** from **page 124–125** according to the 3-point scale.

Mirror Practice — Angry Faces

Using a mirror, have students practice making different intensity angry faces.

3-Point Scale — Scared

Repeat the steps above creating a 3-point scale for scared. Use a word such as worried, uneasy or concerned to describe feeling a little scared. Use a word such as terrified, frightened or horrified to describe feeling very scared.

Read the **Intensity Scenarios—Scared** on **page 114** and have students sort them.

Recognizing Intensity in Facial Expressions

Have students sort the **Scared Facial Expression Cards** from **pages 126–127** according to the 3-point scale.

Mirror Practice — Scared Faces

Using a mirror, have students practice making different intensity scared faces.

Sorting More Facial Expressions

Selecting some of the **Facial Expression Cards** from **pages 57–66** and **120–127** or other pictures you have from magazines or comics, have students sort pictures into the 12 categories (such as: pleased, happy, terrific—blue, sad, miserable—bothered, angry, furious—worried, scared, and terrified).

Making 3-Point Scale Posters

Have each student make his or her own 3-point scale poster for each of the basic emotions. Either provide copies of pictures from this curriculum, provide pictures from other sources or have students draw their own illustrations.

How Happy Are You?
Terrific!
Happy
Glad

Feeling Happy (Sad, Angry, Scared) for Different Reasons

Discuss how there are many different reasons that a person may feel happy, having students provide examples. As students describe situations, use appropriate feeling words (at student's level) that describe that feeling. For example, if a student describes feeling sad because a friend's party was canceled, then you might say he felt disappointed, which is a word that describes feeling sad for a particular reason. Write the new feeling words on the board listing the words under one of the basic feeling words (happy, sad, angry or scared). Refer to the **List of Feeling Words** provided on **page 115**.

Read About Emotions

Read aloud books that describe different intensities of emotions, choosing from the suggested books below or others. Ask students to describe times when they have felt these emotions.

▶ Apel, M. (2002) *Let's Talk About Feeling Defeated.* New York: PowerKids Press. (primary)

▶ Berry, J. (2000). *Let's Talk About Feeling Disappointed.* AZ: Gold Star Publications. (primary)

▶ Berry, J. (2000). *Let's Talk About Feeling Frustrated.* AZ: Gold Star Publications. (primary)

▶ Berry, J. (2000). *Let's Talk About Feeling Worried.* AZ: Gold Star Publications. (primary)

▶ Carlson, N. (1982). *Harriet's Recital.* Minneapolis, MN: Carolrhoda Books, Inc. (primary – a good story to describe different intensities of feeling worried, frightened and terrified)

▶ Crary, E. (1992). *I'm Frustrated.* Seattle, WA: Parenting Press. (primary)

▶ Crary, E. (1993). *I'm Furious.* Seattle, WA: Parenting Press (primary)

▶ Kent, S. (2000). *Let's Talk About Feeling Nervous.* New York: The Rosen Publishing Group, Inc. (primary)

▶ Mayer, M. (2002) *Just Not Invited.* New York: Golden Books Publishing Company. (primary)

▶ Waber, B. (1988). *Ira Says Goodbye.* New York: Scholastic Inc. (primary-intermediate)

▶ Hopkinson, D. (2004). *A Packet of Seeds.* New York: Greenwillow Books. (intermediate)

Dictionary of Emotions

Provide copies of the illustrations that show the least and most intense facial expressions presented above. (The pictures representing #1 and #3 on the 3-point scales). Have students place one picture on each page and write the word that matches the expression. Then have students describe or draw a picture of a situation when someone would feel that way and place each page in their Dictionary of Emotions, placing in alphabetical order if appropriate.

Fun and Games: Additional Learning Activities

Dice Game

Set up a dice game as describe in **Unit 2, page 74**, except replace the words happy, sad, angry, scared and neutral with five of the words chosen to describe intensity of emotions (glad, terrific, annoyed, etc.). Repeat the game, using the remaining words chosen to describe intensity of emotions, repeating some words if needed.

Intensity Charades

Students will use the 3-point scale posters created in the **Teaching Activities, page 105**. When it is the student's turn, he will hold up one of his 3-point scale posters to indicate what type of emotion he is going to demonstrate. He will then demonstrate one of the emotions from the poster, such as looking worried, from the scared 3-point scale. Other students will attempt to guess which of the three emotions he is demonstrating.

Intensity Lotto

Make multiple copies of the **Lotto Game Card** from **page 43** and glue each one on a piece of poster board. Write the words chosen to describe different intensities in random order on the lotto boards, making each board different.

Place the **Facial Expression Cards — Emotional Intensity (pages 120–127)** or other pictures face down or in a container. Either draw and show a card to students or have students take turns drawing the cards. After each card is drawn, students place a marker on the corresponding word on their lotto board.

Treasure Hunt

Using picture books, magazines, comics or other sources, have students search for examples of faces that show low and high intensity emotions, such as a face that looks pleased and one that looks very happy and excited.

Movie Time

While watching a movie, pause and note the different intensity of emotions.

Cross Curricular Activities

Vocabulary Building

Choose some of the additional **Intensity Feeling Words** from the list on **page 115**. Write the words on cards, one word per card. Display the cards on the board. Ask volunteers to read each word aloud and tell what it means. Ask students to sort the cards into four groups—words that express happiness, sadness, anger or fear, placing all the words from one group together.

Writing

Choose some of the intensity feeling words and have students write about a time when they felt that way.

Synonyms

Have students take two sheets of paper and divide each paper into two sections. At the top of each section, have students write the basic feeling words—happy, sad, angry and scared.

Explain to students that synonyms are words that mean about the same thing and instruct them to write as many synonyms as they can under each basic feeling word.

Using a Thesaurus

After completing the activity above, have students locate other synonyms by using a thesaurus.

Art — Drawing or Cartooning

Have students draw faces that show that a person is feeling:

▶ pleased   ▶ bothered   ▶ excited   ▶ furious

▶ disappointed   ▶ worried   ▶ miserable   ▶ terrified

Provide drawings or photos for students to refer to. Other feeling words may be substituted which better match students' vocabulary. If needed, use phrases such as 'a little happy' and 'very happy.'

Read Aloud

During daily read aloud times, pause and discuss the character's feelings at emotional highpoints of the story. Emphasize how emotions change in intensity.

Independent Reinforcement Activities

Activity Sheets

Make copies of the **Activity Sheets 117–119** for students to complete. Some activity pages use Word Banks that can be filled in with the feeling words selected for use in this unit. Others provide common feeling words that represent different intensity. Check to make sure that students are familiar with all the words used on the activity sheets.

Folder Tasks and Work Systems

The following matching and sorting tasks can be used in work systems or folder tasks.

▶ Match pictures of faces with emotion words, such as worried, concerned, furious, etc.

▶ Match a written statement or description—such as "My mom is usually home by now. I wonder what happened?"—with an emotion word such as "worried."

▶ Match a written statement or description ("I wish that guy on the cell phone would be quiet.") with a picture of a face that matches.

It finally stopped raining, so you can play outside.

You just got the best birthday present ever.

You play a game with a friend and win.

You just became friends with someone you really like.

You just got a new puppy.

You get to go see your favorite team play.

You just got a new video game (CD, DVD) that you've wanted for a long time.

Your favorite TV show is on tonight.

You just met your favorite movie star.

You're going out for ice cream.

You and your friend made up after having a big fight.

You get to go to a big water park with lots of water slides.

Your report card is much better than you thought it would be.

You won $500 and you get to spend it on whatever you want.

It finally stopped raining outside.

Your grandfather died.

Your friend can't come over tonight.

You lost your wallet that had a lot of money in it.

You can't play outside with your friends because it's raining.

Your pet died.

You're sick and missed the school fieldtrip.

You didn't get as good a grade on your report as you thought you would.

Your best friend is moving away.

Your parent can't take you to the carnival this weekend.

You dropped the ice cream cone you were eating.

You get a hole in the knee of your new pants.

You weren't invited to another kid's party.

Your parents are going to get a divorce.

You see a stray cat that looks really sick and hungry.

The assembly that was planned for today was cancelled.

A fly keeps buzzing around your face.

You get punished for something you didn't do.

You got splashed by someone in the swimming pool.

Someone is spreading untrue rumors about you.

Your friend keeps saying the same thing over and over.

Your parents won't let you go to see a movie you want to see.

Some kids steal your money.

At the movie theater, someone keeps talking while you are trying to watch a movie.

Someone laughs at you when you trip.

Another student tries to get you in trouble by telling the teacher something you said.

You can't figure out how to do the math assignment.

Some kids deliberately kicked over the sandcastle you built.

Your friend borrowed money and hasn't paid it back.

You can't get the wrapper on your candy bar open.

Your friend forgot the game he said he would loan to you.

The principal keeps looking at you.

You have to sing solo in front of the whole school.

You're afraid you won't do well on a test.

You're home alone at night and you hear strange noises.

You're afraid the teacher will call on you and you don't know the answer.

You are waiting in line to ride the world's tallest rollercoaster.

You're lost in the woods and can't find your way out.

You have to give a report in front of the class.

You're walking in the woods and see a poisonous snake.

A bully has threatened to beat you up.

You're reading a scary story.

Your friend was supposed to call when she got home, but she hasn't called yet.

There's an escaped tiger loose in your neighborhood.

Your parent will be upset because you're late getting home.

You did your homework, but can't find it when you get to school.

Feeling Words

Intensity and Variations of Basic Emotions

(with approximate reading level of word)

Happy	Angry	Sad	Scared
glad (K)	mad (K)	down (K)	afraid (1st)
happy (K)	angry (1st)	hurt (K)	fearful (1st)
great (K)	cross (1st)	let down (K)	nervous (1st)
pleased (K)	bothered (2nd)	low (K)	scared (1st)
silly (1st)	fuming (3rd)	sad (K)	worried (1st)
thankful (1st)	upset (3rd)	blue (1st)	alarmed (3rd)
proud (2nd)	furious (4th)	grumpy (1st)	concerned (3rd)
content (3rd)	agitated (5th)	left out (1st)	terrified (3rd)
delighted (3rd)	annoyed (5th)	troubled (1st)	anxious (4th)
good mood (3rd)	distressed (5th)	unhappy (1st)	startled (4th)
excited (4th)	frustrated (5th)	hopeless (2nd)	suspicious (4th)
thrilled (4th)	enraged (6th)	lonely (2nd)	uneasy (4th)
terrific (5th)		gloomy (3rd)	cautious (5th)
ecstatic (6th)		miserable (4th)	frightened (5th)
exhilarated (6th)		defeated (5th)	horrified (5th)
		depressed (5th)	panicked (5th)
		disappointed (5th)	threatened (5th)
		discouraged (5th)	
		grieving (5th)	
		rejected (5th)	
		desolate (6th)	

Other Feeling Words

Kindergarten

kind

loved

shy

sick

First Grade

brave

doubtful

important

interested

shocked

surprised

Second Grade

bored

hopeful

joyful

proud

sorry

tired

Third Grade

bitter

calm

cheerful

concerned

curious

helpless

moody

satisfied

shamed

Fourth Grade

affectionate

amused

ashamed

astonished

bashful

confused

disapproving

enthusiastic

envious

exhausted

grateful

greedy

guilty

hesitant

insecure

inspired

mischievous

pressured

puzzled

relieved

responsible

sympathetic

Fifth Grade

amazed

contempt

desperate

determined

disgusted

distressed

eager

embarrassed

impressed

indifferent

jealous

obstinate

regretful

resentful

tense

timid

threatened

triumphant

Sixth Grade

aggressive

anguished

apologetic

arrogant

assertive

awed

confident

disturbed

negative

perplexed

remorseful

stressed

Grade level approximations taken from *Children's Writer's Word Book* (1992) by Alijandra Mogilner, Writer's Digest Books, Cinninati, OH.

Name_____

What are they feeling?

Write a word from the Word Bank that matches each picture using the words below.

_____ _____ _____

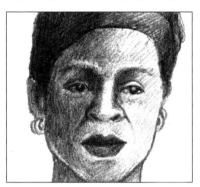

_____ _____ _____

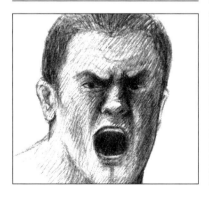

_____ _____ _____

Use the words provided or cut on dotted line and provide other words.

Word Bank

terrified	upset	troubled
glad	hopeless	delighted
let down	afraid	furious

What are they thinking?

Draw a line from the face to the matching thought.

"Sometimes it bugs me when people talk on their cell phones."

"Wow! This is the best birthday present ever!"

"That makes me so mad I feel like punching him!"

"I wonder what time it is."

"Oh good. It's time for lunch."

Name_____

Different Words for Feeling Different

Write words from the Word Bank on each feeling scale.

↑ More Happy

_____

_____

_____

Less Happy

↑ More Angry

_____

_____

_____

Less Angry

↑ More Sad

_____

_____

_____

Less Sad

↑ More Scared

_____

_____

_____

Less Scared

- -

Use the words provided or cut on dotted line and provide other words.

Word Bank

blue	glad	alarmed
pleased	bothered	mad
miserable	furious	excited
troubled	worried	uneasy

Cartoons—Happy Faces

Drawings—Happy Faces

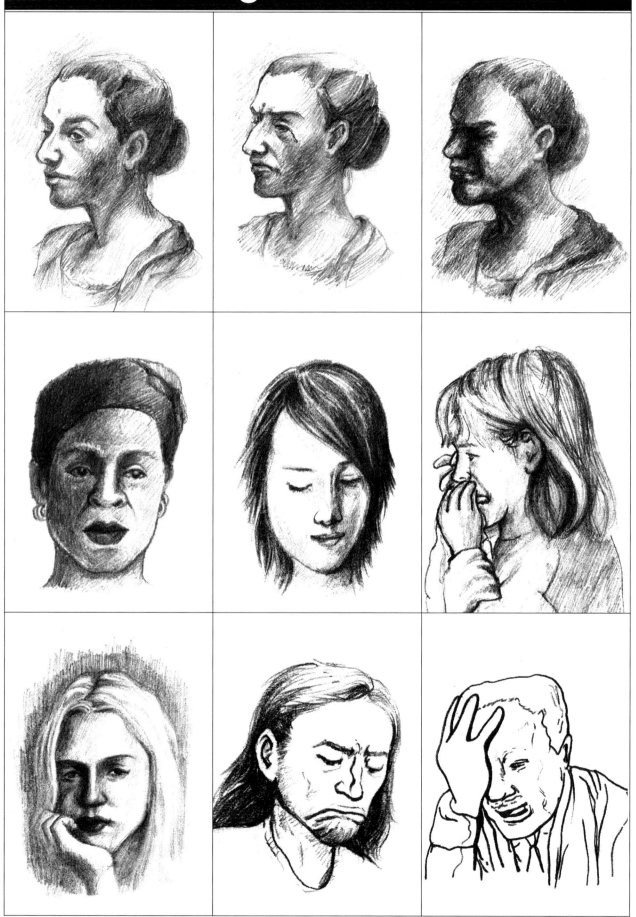

Drawings—Angry Faces

Getting the Message: Learning to Read Facial Expressions | **Emotional Intensity Face Picture Cards** |

Drawings—Scared Faces

UNIT 4
Other Emotions

Teaching Activities

Interested or Bored?

▶ Ask a student volunteer to talk to you about a topic and to watch what your face looks like while she is talking. Ask other students to watch your face as well. You could select a topic for the student, such as favorite TV shows or what she did over the weekend, or have the student select a topic. As the student talks to you, act interested; look at the student, change your facial expressions to correspond to what is being said, look alert and attentive, nod occasionally, perhaps tilt your head to one side, etc.

▶ Ask students if they thought you looked interested and have them describe what they observed. Make a list of the facial expressions they noted — looking at the speaker, possibly smiling, nodding or tilting head. (Students may also note body language. Make note of body language, but try to key in on the head and face.)

▶ Repeat this activity with the same or a different student, this time looking bored and not interested; look away, don't change facial expressions to correspond to what is being said, maintain a dull, disinterested look or change facial expressions to correspond with internal thoughts or other things that are happening in the environment.

▶ Ask students if they thought you looked interested or bored and have them describe what they observed. Again, make a list of the facial expressions noted.

Mirror Practice

Using mirrors have students practice looking interested, using the facial expressions noted in the Interested or Bored activity.

I'm Interested in What You Have to Say

▶ Demonstrate for students how a person who is talking makes signals to another person that it is his turn to speak (stop talking, turn face towards person, make eye contact, raise eyebrows).

▶ Make copies of the **It's Your Turn Scripts, page 143** and distribute to students. Pair up students and have them read the It's Your Turn conversations. Each listener should practice looking interested and each speaker should practice the appropriate signals each time she finishes speaking.

▶ Have students carry on brief conversations using the following or other topics, demonstrating interest and signaling the other person's turn to speak. Remind students to make a brief statement, then ask a question of their conversation partner.

- What they did over the weekend

- What they will do after school

- What are their favorite TV shows

- How they like to spend their free time

- What is their favorite part of the school day

To Smile or Not to Smile

Discuss how smiling sometimes is a good way to show interest and sometimes not, depending on what the other person is saying and what he is feeling. Explain that if the speaker is sad or upset, and the listener is smiling, the speaker will feel that the listener isn't listening, doesn't care or is making fun of the speaker. Read the following statements and have students demonstrate whether they, as listeners would smile or not.

▶ "I had so much fun last night! Guess what I did?"

▶ "I'm really worried about how I did on that test."

▶ "It's so sad. My dog is getting so old he can barely walk anymore."

▶ "I've got to tell you this joke my brother told me."

▶ "I'm really not feeling well at all."

▶ "They're going to show some of my drawings at the art show."

▶ "That big kid over there keeps picking on me."

▶ "I'm so awful at sports. I hate PE."

▶ "I really don't get how to do these math problems."

▶ "Want to come over and play video games after school?"

Interested or Bored Card Sort

Copy and cut out the **Interested and Bored Facial Expression Cards, page 158–160**. Have students sort the cards.

Dictionary of Emotions

Provide copies of one bored and one interested face from the **Interested and Bored Expression Cards pages 158–160**. Have students place one picture on each page and write the word that matches the expression. Then, on each page, ask students to write a description or draw a picture of a situation when someone would feel that way, then place the pages in alphabetical order and create a "Dictionary of Emotions."

Feeling Disgusted

▶ Ask students to imagine that they are eating eating lunch when someone threw up on the table, or was making gross burping noises. Ask students how witnessing those behaviors would make them feel. Introduce the word 'disgusted' if necessary and write the word 'disgusted' on the board.

▶ Ask students to give examples of situations that might make someone feel disgusted or examples of times they have felt disgusted.

▶ Give each student a copy of a **Disgusted Face** from **page 163**. Ask students to describe how a person looks when she is disgusted (eyes partly shut in a squint, eyebrows lowered and squeezed towards nose, mouth frowning, nose wrinkled).

▶ Have students place the picture on a sheet of paper, write the word disgusted on the paper and describe or draw a picture of a situation when someone would feel disgusted. Students then place the page in their Dictionary of Emotions.

Mirror Practice — Disgusted

Have students practice looking disgusted while watching themselves in the mirror.

Sincere or Fake?

▶ Discuss how sometimes people will pretend to be happy or pleased when they really aren't. Review how the different parts of the face look when someone is happy (the mouth is smiling, cheeks pushed up, eyebrows up, not lowered). Explain that often when someone is pretending to be happy their mouth will smile, but their eyes don't. The lips will form a smile, but the cheeks don't go up and their eyes may be looking down. Or, their smile may be crooked.

▶ Show pictures from **page 161 (Sincere and Smiling)** and from **page 162 (Smiling, Not Happy)**.

▶ Ask students to tell how the faces differ. Explain that the Not Happy faces may have sad eyes or a mean look. With older students you might want to introduce the words 'smug' or 'contempt' to describe the feeling that goes with some of the faces.

▶ Demonstrate some insincere smiling faces and ask students to imitate them. Ask students how they feel when they are making the face. Do they feel happy or do they feel upset or mean?

Mirror Practice Faking It

Have students practice making genuine and insincere smiling faces while watching themselves in the mirror.

Happy or Fake?

Copy and cut out the **Sincere and Smiling, Not Happy Expression Cards** from **pages 161–162**. Have students take turns drawing a card and deciding if the expression is sincere or not really happy.

Dictionary of Emotions

Provide copies of a couple of Smiling, Not Happy Face cards from page 162. Include a sad smile and a fake smile. Have students place one picture on each page and write a phrase that matches the expression (such as smiling, but really sad or smiling, but not happy or fake smile). Then, on each page, have students write a description or draw a picture of a situation when someone would smile, but not actually be happy. Have students place the pages into their Dictionary of Emotions.

Feeling Embarrassed

▶ Ask students to imagine that they were walking up in front of the whole school and tripped and fell down or they were called on in class and gave the wrong answer and everyone laughed. If necessary, introduce the word, 'embarrassed.'

▶ Write the word 'embarrassed' on the board. Explain that people feel embarrassed when they are upset because of what others might think or feel about them.

▶ Ask students to give examples of situations that might make someone feel embarrassed. Ask for volunteers to tell about a time when they felt embarrassed.

▶ Give each student a copy of an **Embarrassed Face** from **page 166**. Ask students to describe how a person looks when he is embarrassed (eyes averted, tense smile, blushing). Many emotions, including embarrassment are not as easy to recognize just by looking at the face. What could be embarrassment, could also be shyness or self-satisfaction. So, students may have more difficulty in both recognizing and describing these emotions. Body language and what's going on are often necessary to read theses emotions. The important thing is to help students become aware of facial expressions and what the different possible emotions are.

▶ Have students place the picture on a page, write the word embarrassment and describe or draw a picture of a situation when someone would feel embarrassed. The page is then placed in their Dictionary of Emotions.

▶ Read books about feeling embarrassed. See list on pages 137–138 for suggestions.

Mirror Practice — Embarrassed

Have students try to look embarrassed while watching themselves in the mirror.

Feeling Shy, Feeling Confident

▶ Ask students to imagine they are at a party where they don't know hardly anyone, or they are speaking in front of a group of strangers, or a similar type of situation. How would they feel? Students will likely say that they would feel scared. Ask students why they would feel scared since they know that nothing is going to harm them. Students will likely respond that they are afraid of either being embarrassed or rejected.

▶ Write the word 'shy' on the board and tell students that when someone is feeling afraid of what others will think of them, that person is feeling shy. Explain that everyone feels shy sometimes, and some people feel shy more often than others. Write the word 'confident' on the board and explain that feeling confident is the opposite of feeling shy.

▶ Ask students to describe times when they have felt shy.

▶ Provide students with a copy of a picture of a **Shy Face** from **page 166**. Ask students to describe how a person looks when she is feeling shy (down cast eyes or eyes averted, slight smile, may be blushing).

▶ Provide students with a copy of a **Confident Face** from **page 164**. Ask students to describe how a person looks when he or she looks confident (chin up, looking happy).

▶ Have students place the pictures on separate pages and on each page write the word that matches the expression and describe or draw a picture of a situation when someone would feel that way. Then place the pages in their Dictionary of Emotions.

▶ Read books about feeling shy. See list on pages 137–138.

Shy or Confident?

Randomly select scenarios from pages 146–147 (under "Shy" and "Confident") and read to students. Have students choose the correct feeling..

Mirror Practice — Shy and Confident

Have students practice trying to look shy and confident while watching themselves in the mirror.

Feeling Sorry or Ashamed

▶ Ask students to imagine that they were caught cheating on a test or were poking fun of a friend when that friend walked up from behind and heard what was said. Ask students how they would feel, and if necessary introduce the words 'sorry' or 'ashamed.'

▶ Write the words 'sorry' or 'ashamed' on the board. Explain that people feel sorry or ashamed when they do something they know was wrong or hurtful and regret doing it.

▶ Ask students to give examples of situations that might make someone feel sorry or ashamed. Ask for volunteers to tell about a time when they felt sorry or ashamed.

▶ Give students a copy of an **Ashamed Face** from **page 166**. Ask students to describe how a person looks when he or she is ashamed (eyes cast down, looking sad).

▶ Have students place the picture on a page, write the word that matches the expression, describe or draw a picture of a situation when someone would feel sorry or ashamed, then place the page in their Dictionary of Emotions.

▶ Read books about feeling sorry or ashamed. See the list on pages 137–138.

Mirror Practice — Ashamed or Sorry

Have students practice looking ashamed or sorry while watching themselves in the mirror.

Feeling Jealous

▶ Ask students to imagine that someone they know always has a lots of friends, always has cool new clothes, the latest video games, etc., and other people are always paying attention to that person and not to you. Ask students how they would feel and if necessary introduce the word 'jealous' or 'envious.'

▶ Write the words, 'jealous' on the board. Explain that people feel jealous or envious when they want what someone else has and they feel a little angry that another person has it and they don't.

▶ Ask students to give examples of situations when someone might feel jealous or envious. Ask for volunteers to tell about a time when they felt jealous.

▶ Provide students with a copy of a **Jealous Face** from **page 163**. Ask students to describe how a person might look when he is jealous (angry or smiling but looking mean). Point out, however, that some people can feel jealous, but not show it in their facial expressions.

▶ Have students place the picture on a page, write the word jealous and describe or draw a picture of a situation when someone would feel jealous. Then place the page in their Dictionary of Emotions.

▶ Read books about feeling jealous. See list on page 137–138.

Mirror Practice — Jealous

Have students try to look jealous while watching themselves in the mirror.

Feeling Confused

▶ Ask students to imagine that they were given a homework assignment that doesn't make any sense or their friend is really mad at them, but they don't know why. Ask students how they would feel and if necessary introduce the word 'confused.'

▶ Write the word, 'confused' on the board. Explain that people feel confused when they don't understand what's happening or what they're supposed to do.

▶ Give students a copy of a **Confused Face** from **page 164**. Ask students to describe how a person might look when she is confused (worried look, head cocked sideways, forehead creased, eyebrows pushed towards nose).

▶ Have students add a page about feeling confused to their Dictionary of Emotions.

▶ Read books about feeling confused. See list on pages 137–138.

Mirror Practice — Confused

Have students practice looking confused while watching themselves in the mirror.

Feeling Surprised, Feeling Doubtful

▶ Ask students to imagine that when they got home from school they had received an unexpected present in the mail or they woke up in the morning and it had snowed unexpectedly. Ask students how they would feel and if necessary introduce the word 'surprised.'

▶ Write the word 'surprised' on the board. Explain that people feel surprised when something unexpected happens. Usually what happens is something the person likes or something that doesn't matter, but is unexpected. If something bad happens unexpectedly, the person is more likely to feel angry or frightened.

▶ Now ask students how they would feel if a friend came and told them that a famous rock star or sports figure called them on the phone last night. First, they might feel surprised, but soon they would probably doubt what their friend had told them. They would feel 'doubtful' or 'skeptical.' Write the word 'doubtful' on the board.

▶ Ask students to give examples of when a person might feel surprised and when they might be doubtful. Ask for volunteers to tell about times they experienced those feelings.

▶ Give students a copy of a **Surprised Face** from **page 165**. Ask students to describe how a person might look when he or she is surprised (eyes wide open, eyebrows raised, and mouth open — similar to fear except without the tension and the eyebrows do not push towards the nose).

▶ Give students a copy of a **Doubtful Face** from **page 165**. Ask students to describe how a person might look when he or she is doubtful (chin tucked in, head may be tilted, crooked smile, eyebrows lowered).

▶ Have students add these expressions to their Dictionary of Emotions.

Surprised or Doubtful?

Randomly select scenarios from pages 149–150 and read to students. Have students tell what they are feeling.

Mirror Practice — Surprised

Have students practice looking surprised while watching themselves in the mirror. They might try looking doubtful as well.

Caring About Others, Feeling Concern

▶ Ask students to imagine that their best friend is very sad because his pet just died. How would they feel? Then ask them to imagine that their best friend was very excited because she just won first prize in a contest, or that someone was picking on their friend. How would they feel?

▶ Write the words 'caring about others' and 'concern' on the board. Explain that when a person cares about someone they share what the other person is feeling to a degree. When your friend is sad, you are sad and want to help your friend feel better. And when your friend is happy, you feel happy for them. When your friend is upset, you are upset. When you care about someone who is upset, you are feeling 'concern.' Ask students to give examples of caring about and feeling concern for others.

▶ Provide students with a copy of the pictures **Concerned Faces** from **page 167**. Ask students to describe how the people look in the different scenes. Point out that the facial expressions of the concerned listeners are similar to the facial expressions of their friends. When you are concerned about someone, you will copy his facial expressions.

▶ Have students place one or more of the pictures on a page, write the words 'Caring About Others,' and describe what the people in the picture are feeling and place the page in the Dictionary of Emotions. An alternative would be to draw a picture of someone showing concern for another.

Act It Out

Pair up students and give each pair of students the **Acting It Out—Showing Concern** on **page 152.** Have students take turns reading the quotes while the other student shows concern.

Fun and Games: Additional Learning Activities

Read About Emotions

Read aloud books that describe different emotions, discussing the emotions.

▶ Aliki, (1984). *Feelings.* New York: Greenwillow Books. (primary)

▶ Anholt, C. (1994). *What Makes Me Happy?* Cambridge, MA: Candlewick Press. (primary)

▶ Avery, C. (1992). *Everybody Has Feelings: Todos Tenemos Sentimientos.* Seattle, WA: Open Hand Publishing, Inc. (primary)

► Cain, J. (2000). *The Way I Feel.* Seattle, WA: Parenting Press, Inc. (primary)

► Colin, S. (1989). *Let's Talk About Feelings: Ellie's Day.* Seattle, WA: Parenting Press, Inc. (primary)

► Curtis, J. (1998) *Today I Feel Silly & Other Moods That Make My Day.* New York: Joanna Cotler Books. (primary)

► Johnston, M. (1996). *Let's Talk About Being Shy.* New York: The Rosen Publishing Group, Inc. (primary)

► Kachenmeister, C. (1989). *On Monday When It Rained.* New York: Houghton Mifflin Company. (primary)

► Apel, M. (2001). *Let's Talk About Being Embarrassed.* New York: The Rosen Publishing Group, Inc. (primary-intermediate)

► Apel, M. (2001). *Let's Talk About Feeling Confused.* New York: The Rosen Publishing Group, Inc. (primary-intermediate)

► Polacco, P. (1994). *Tikvah Means Hope.* New York: A Doubleday Book for Young Readers. (primary–intermediate)

► Polacco, P. (1998). *Thank You Mr. Falker.* New York: Philomel Books. (primary–intermediate)

► Braithwaite, A. (1998). *Feeling Jealous.* Milwaukee, WI: Gareth Stevens Publishing. (primary–intermediate)

► Braithwaite, A. (1998). *Feeling Shy.* Milwaukee, WI: Gareth Stevens Publishing. (primary–intermediate)

► Lugwig, T. (2004). *My Secret Bully.* Berkeley, CA: Tricycle Press. (intermediate)

► Polacco, P. (1994). *Pink and Say.* New York: Philomel Books. (intermediate)

Charades with Different Emotions

Choose feeling words that students have in their Dictionary of Emotions and write them on cards, one on each card. You may choose to limit the number of words used. Write the words to be used on the board for students to refer to. Students take turns drawing a card and making that expression and attempt to guess which facial expression they are displaying.

To make a competitive game, divide students into teams having teammates attempting to guess the facial expressions of other teammates while you keep track of how long it takes for the team to guess the correct answer. The team with the least total guessing time wins.

Sunday Funnies

Using easily understood comic strips (see suggested **Sunday Funnies** on **page 39**), make transparencies and discuss what is happening in the comic, what the characters are feeling and their facial expressions.

Dice Game

Have students write one of the following lists of feeling words on a piece of paper or on cards, one on each card. Divide students into small groups, giving each group one die. Students take turns rolling the die. The student will then tell about a time she felt an emotion, depending on the number rolled. (See below.) After the student answers, then she can cross out that emotion or turn over the card. Whoever crosses out all the emotion words first, or turns over all of her cards wins.

1. interested	1. confident	1. insincere
2. bored	2. sorry	2. surprised
3. disgusted	3. ashamed	3. doubtful
4. embarrassed	4. jealous	4. concern
5. shy	5. confused	5. envious

Emotions Lotto

Make multiple copies of the **Lotto Game Card** from **page 43** and glue each one on a piece of poster boards. Write the feelings words from this unit in random order on the lotto boards, making each board different.

Place the **Facial Expression Cards — Other Emotions (pages 158–167)** face down or in a container. Either draw a card and show it to students or have students take turns drawing the cards. After each card is drawn, students place a marker on the corresponding word on their lotto board.

Name That Emotion

Have several "contestants" compete at a time. Read a scenario from **Scenarios—Other Emotions, page 144–151** and have students raise their hands to name the emotion. First hand up gets to answer. Keep score and the first person to score five wins.

Movie Time

Watch a movie with lots of emotional ups and downs and pause and discuss what the characters are feeling. *Mr. Bean* movies and TV shows provide a variety of easy to read facial expressions.

Show that Emotion

Randomly pick scenarios from **Scenarios—Other Emotions, page 144–151** and read them to students. Have students show the appropriate facial expressions, using mirrors if needed.

Pleasant and Uncomfortable Feelings

Choose feeling words that students have in their Dictionary of Emotions and write them on cards, one on each card. Write the word 'pleasant' on one side of the board and the word 'uncomfortable' on the other side.

Discuss how when some feelings are pleasant, we like them and why others make us feel uncomfortable to various degrees. Next, have students take turns drawing a card and placing the card under either 'pleasant' or 'uncomfortable.'

Read and Pause

Read aloud a book that expresses a variety of more complex emotions. (See suggested books listed below.) After each emotional event, stop reading and ask students what the character is most likely to be feeling and have them demonstrate how the character's face might look.

- ▶ Robberecht, (2003). *Angry Dragon.* New York: Clarion Books. (primary)

- ▶ Spinelli, E. (2006). *Somebody Loves You Mr. Hatch.* New York: Simon & Schuster Children's Publishing. (primary)

- ▶ Hoffman, M. (1991). *Amazing Grace.* New York: Dial Books for Young Readers. (primary–intermediate)

- ▶ Hopkins, L. (2005). *Oh, No! Where Are My Pants? And Other Disasters: Poems.* New York: Haper Collins Children's Books. (primary-intermediate)

- ▶ Polacco, P. (1994). *My Rotten Redheaded Older Brother.* New York: Simon & Schuster Books for Young Readers. (primary–intermediate)

- ▶ Bunting, E. (1994). *Smoky Night.* Orlando, Fl: Harcourt Brace & Co. (intermediate)

- ▶ Bunting, E. (1996). *Going Home.* New York: Joanna Cotler Books. (intermediate)

- ▶ McKissack, P. (2001). *Goin' Someplace Special.* New York: Atheneum Books for Young Readers. (intermediate)

- ▶ Rylant, C. (1983). *Miss Maggie.* New York: E.P. Dutton, Inc. (intermediate)

- ▶ Say, A. (1999). *Tea with Milk.* New York: Walter Lorraine Books. (intermediate)

Cross Curricular Activities

Write About It

Have students complete the following or similar types of sentences.

▶ One thing that really interests me is...

▶ A time I felt bored was when...

▶ A time I felt disgusted was when...

▶ A time I saw someone smile who was not really happy was when...

▶ A time I felt embarrassed was when...

▶ A time I felt shy was when...

▶ A time I felt confident was when...

▶ A time I felt sorry was when...

▶ A time I felt ashamed was when...

▶ A time I felt surprised was when...

▶ A time I felt doubtful was when...

▶ A time I felt concern for someone was when...

▶ A time someone showed concern for me was when...

Reading — Find the Feeling

Provide the students with a list or partial list of the feeling words covered in this unit (interested, bored, disgusted, etc.) before they begin reading a story. Have students write down the page number that indicates when a character in the story felt that emotion.

Reading and Graphic Organizers

Make copies and distribute the **Story Organizer** on **page 93** or use a similar type of graphic organizer. As Students complete their reading, have them fill in what happened and what the characters felt.

Act It Out

Incorporate a little drama as part of your reading program by having students act out stories or parts of stories that they have read, or use short plays written at the appropriate reading level. Discuss how the character would feel and emphasize using appropriate facial expressions.

Art with Feeling

Have students draw, paint or create collages depicting different emotions.

Art Appreciation

Examine famous works of art, as described in Units 1 and 2, including discussion of the emotions presented in this unit.

Read Aloud

During daily read aloud times, pause and discuss the character's feelings at emotional highpoints of the story.

Independent Reinforcement Activities

Activity Sheets

Make copies of the **Activity Sheets 153–157** and have students complete.

Folder Tasks and Work Systems

The following matching and sorting tasks can be used in work systems or folder tasks.

- ► Match feeling words with pictures
- ► Sort feeling words into pleasant and uncomfortable feelings
- ► Match a scenario with a facial expression
- ► Match a thought with a facial expression, such as "Oh! I wish I hadn't said that," with a face with an embarrassed looking expression.

Read the scripts with your partner. When you finish reading your part, turn and look at the other speaker to signal that it's his or her turn to talk. When the other speaker is talking, try to make your face look interested.

At Break Time
(**Scene:** 2 students at recess or on break)

Speaker 1: "We went to the game on Saturday. It was a lot of fun. Did you do anything fun this weekend?"

Speaker 2: "No. I just laid around all weekend. I was sick. Who won the game?"

Speaker 1: "Our team won. It wasn't even close. We just wiped them out. That's too bad you were sick. What was the matter?"

Speaker 2: "I guess it was just a bad cold, I was really tired, but I feel OK now. Want to go shoot some baskets?"

Speaker 1: "Sure."

After the Movie
(**Scene:** 2 kids coming out of the theater after a movie)

Speaker 1: "Wow! That was a great movie. Did you like it?"

Speaker 2: "Yeah, it was pretty good, but I didn't like the ending. I thought it was kind of lame. Did you like the part where they were rescued?"

Speaker 1: "Yeah! Great special effects! You got to admit it was a lot better than that last one we saw."

Speaker 2: "No kidding! That one was so stupid. Where's your mom picking us up?"

New Clothes
(**Scene:** 2 kids during recess or at break)

Speaker 1: "Hey, I like your shirt. Is it new?"

Speaker 2: "Yeah. My mom took me shopping last night. We went to that new store that just opened in the shopping center. Have you been in there yet?"

Speaker 1: "No. I didn't even know it was open yet. Do they have some cool stuff?"

Speaker 2: "Yeah. Some of there stuff's pretty good. Where do you like to shop for clothes?"

Scenarios— Other Emotions

Interested

When there's a football game on TV, Clancy watches every minute of it.
▶ What is Clancy feeling?

Your friend says, "I want to hear all about your trip."
▶ What is your friend feeling?

You weren't planning to watch TV, but this show came on that you couldn't stop watching.
▶ What are you feeling?

You thought the assembly was really good. The time seemed to go by so quickly.
▶ What are you feeling?

As you are telling a friend about your weekend, he listens to you and asks questions.
▶ What is your friend feeling?

Not Interested or Bored

Josh feels like falling asleep when his teacher starts talking about history.
▶ What is Josh feeling?

Whenever you talk to Jenny at lunch, she's always watching other kids and never responds to anything you say.
▶ What is Jenny feeling?

You just asked your friend if he liked the movie, but he went on and on and had to tell you everything that happened in the movie.
▶ What are you feeling?

When Ben was talking to Chris, Chris just kept on looking at the magazine he was reading.

▶ What is Chris feeling?

When Summer told her friend Natalie about a fight she had with her mother, Natalie said, "I guess I'll go home now."

▶ What is Natalie feeling?

Disgusted

You just stepped in dog poop.

▶ What are you feeling?

You cringe every time Jeff cracks his knuckles.

▶ What are you feeling?

Haley doesn't like it when her brother talks about gross things.

▶ How does Haley feel?

Your uncle takes off his shoes, and his feet really smell bad.

▶ How are you feeling?

Your brother burps right in your face.

▶ How do you feel?

Embarrassed

The teacher called on you and you gave the wrong answer.
▶ What are you feeling?

When you looked in the mirror you saw that you had lettuce stuck in your teeth.
▶ What are you feeling?

Amanda fell in the middle of her dance routine.
▶ How did Amanda feel?

Tony forgot some of his lines when he was in the school play.
▶ How did Tony feel?

When you were walking into the classroom, you tripped and fell and everyone was watching.
▶ What are you feeling?

Shy

Kristen never knows what to say when her parents' friends talk to her.
▶ What is Kristen feeling?

Dan feels kind of funny when he's at a party with a lot of people he doesn't know.
▶ What is Dan feeling?

Keisha doesn't like to go up to a group of kids and ask if she can join them.
▶ What is Keisha feeling?

Carrie's baby brother, Bobby, always hides behind Carrie whenever anyone new talks to him.
▶ How does Bobby feel?

It's Emma's first day at a new school. She doesn't know who to sit by at lunch.
▶ What is Emma feeling?

Confident

Jason is looking forward to playing in the band concert because he has practiced and is sure he will play well.
▶ What is Jason feeling?

You feel sure that you did a really good job on the report you wrote.
▶ How do you feel?

Clayton likes meeting new people because he's sure that they will like him.
▶ How does Clayton feel?

Bethany likes her new job and feels that she is a good worker.
▶ What is Bethany feeling?

Jeremy feels sure he will meet his goals.
▶ How is Jeremy feeling?

Sorry or Ashamed

You were joking and hurt your friend's feelings.
▶ What are you feeling?

Emily took some money that didn't belong to her.
▶ What is Emily feeling?

Veronica was in a bad mood and yelled at her best friend for no reason.
▶ How is Veronica feeling?

Eric feels bad because he was caught lying to his parents.
▶ How does Eric feel?

Roy joined some other kids in making fun of the new kid at school, but wishes he hadn't done that.

▶ How does Roy feel?

Jealous

Ashley's friend Brittany was chosen to be on the dance team. Ashley really wanted to be on the team, but wasn't chosen.

▶ How is Ashley feeling?

Amber says, "It's not fair that Jasmine gets the leading part in the play."

▶ What is Amber feeling?

Your friend always seems to have a lot more money to spend than you do.

▶ How would you feel?

Tyler has to study really hard and still doesn't do that well at school, but his brother hardly ever studies and gets really good grades.

▶ How does Tyler feel?

Matt gets upset because his friend is always bragging about all the fun things he does with other kids.

▶ What is Matt feeling?

Confused

Billy says, "I can't figure out how this computer works."
▶ What is Billy feeling?

Henry doesn't know what to think. One of his friends told on him, but they all say they didn't.
▶ What is Henry feeling?

Math is hard for you. It just doesn't seem to make sense.
▶ How are you feeling?

This lady kept trying to tell you something, but she was speaking a different language.
▶ How do you feel?

You're trying to find your way to a new store, but can't figure out where it is.
▶ What are you feeling?

Surprised

Kenny said, "I can't believe I won 1st prize!"
▶ What is Kenny feeling?

Kayla had no idea her friends were planning a surprise party for her.
▶ How did Kayla feel when she found out?

You weren't expecting to see your friend, but there he is!
▶ How are you feeling?

You thought sure you failed the test, but you got an 'A' on it.

▶ What are you feeling?

Scott didn't know his grandfather was coming for a visit, but when he got home, there he was.

▶ What is Scott feeling?

Doubtful

Becca said, "I think you're wrong. Bobby wouldn't say that. You must have misunderstood."

▶ What is Becca feeling?

Cheyenne's friends keep telling her that she won 1st prize, but she thinks they are just kidding her.

▶ How is Cheyenne feeling?

The new kid is telling you that he did all these really exciting things where he lived before, but you think he's just making it up.

▶ How are you feeling?

You see a newspaper in the store that says some dogs have come here from other planets.

▶ How are you feeling?

It's April Fool's Day and you think that your friend is playing a joke.

▶ What are you feeling?

Concerned

Kyle said, "You look kind of pale. Are you feeling OK?"
▶ What is Kyle feeling?

Sarah said, "I'm so sorry that your grandmother is in the hospital. You must be really worried."
▶ What is Sarah feeling?

Your friend is really mad at Derrick who was picking on her.
▶ How are you feeling?

Your friend is really nervous about trying out for the team.
▶ What are you feeling?

You can tell that your friend is worried, but you don't know why.
▶ What are you feeling?

Act It Out— Showing Concern

Take turns reading the following quotes, while the listener shows interest and concern.

1. "I've got a great idea! Want to hear it?"

2. "I'm so mad at my brother. He's always bullying me and making fun of me!"

3. "Oh no! I can't find my report! I got it done and it's due today, but it's not in my backpack!"

4. "I did it! I made the team!"

5. "I feel so bad. I didn't mean to but I was joking with Aaron and really upset him."

6. "It's just not fair that Samantha always gets to be the leader."

7. "I'm so embarrassed. I really messed up on my lines in the play."

8. "My dog got hit by a car. We took him to the vet, but we don't know if he's going to be OK."

9. "I get to go shopping after school. I can't wait!"

10. "That kid over there tripped me and then laughed."

Name_____

Name that facial expression

Write happy or not really happy to tell how the person is feeling.

_____ _____ _____

_____ _____ _____

_____ _____ _____

What do their faces tell?

Draw a line from the face to the matching description.

does not really believe what you are saying

doesn't understand what you just said

feels proud

is tired or bored

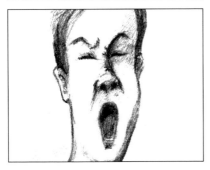

feels sorry

What are they thinking?

Draw a line from the face to the matching thought.

"I can't believe I won 1st prize!"

"I can't stand that smell!"

"I just don't believe that
Andy would do that."

"I don't see why her painting got chosen
for the art show and mine didn't!"

"This is so boring.
I wish he'd stop talking."

Interested or not interested?

Tell if the listener is interested or not interested.

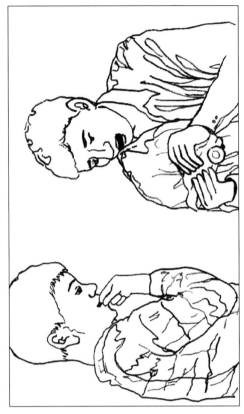

Is he interested?

Is she interested?

Is he interested?

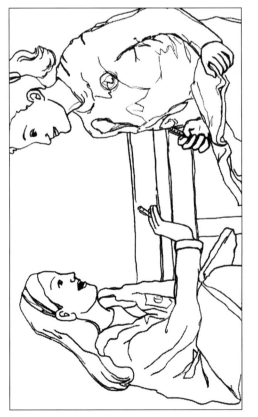

Is she interested?

Getting the Message: Learning to Read Facial Expressions | **Activity Sheet** |

Name the feeling

Choose a word from the Word Bank to tell how you think the person is feeling.
Use each word one time.

_____ 1. Ian just can't understand the directions that came
with the model airplane kit.

_____ 2. Amy dropped her lunch tray on the floor and
everyone stopped eating and turned to look at her.

_____ 3. Trevor reads everything he can about trains.

_____ 4. Kelly gets really quiet when she is around people
she doesn't know.

_____ 5. Jacob borrowed a CD from his friend and lost it.

_____ 6. Noah knows his report card will be good because
he worked really hard.

_____ 7. Belinda wants her friend to do well on a test,
so she helps her study.

_____ 8. Molly doesn't like it when her sister gets all
the attention.

Word Bank

concerned   confident   confused

embarrassed   interested

jealous   shy   sorry

Interested-Bored Faces

Interested Faces

Sincere and Smiling Faces

Smiling, Not Happy Faces

Disgusted and Jealous Faces

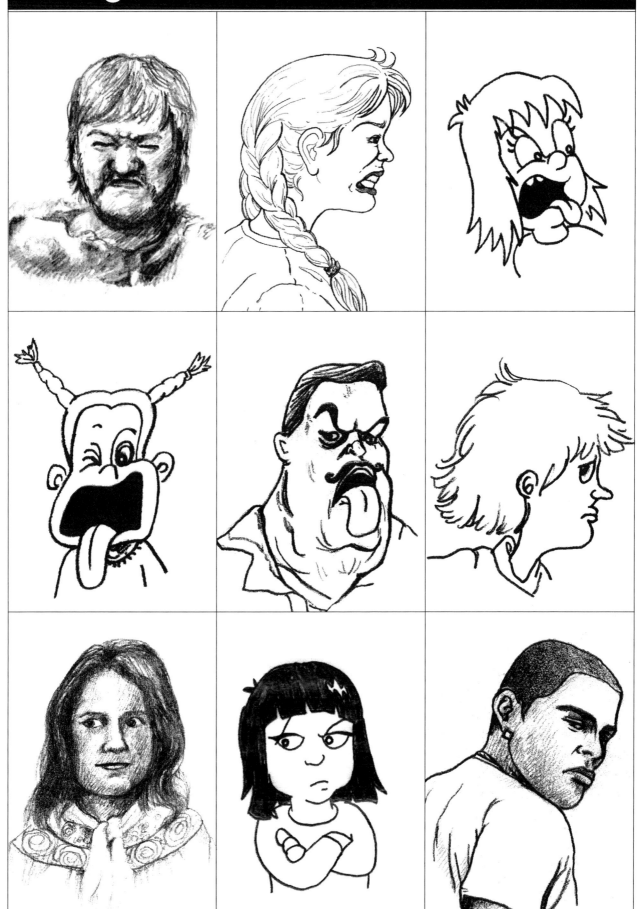

Surprised and Doubtful Faces

Getting the Message: Learning to Read Facial Expressions | **Other Emotion Face Picture Card** |

Concerned Faces